City of Poems

City of Poems

Garrett Buhl Robinson

Poet in the Park ®
In Humanity I see Grace, Beauty and Dignity.

The Merce Cunningham quote in the poem "Blank Page" was heard by the author in the lecture by Justin Tornow: "Cunningham Technique as a Practice of Freedom" at *100 Years of Merce Cunningham: A Symposium of Ideas for the Next Century* at The New York Public Library for the Performing Arts.

Photograph of the author in the back of the book © Bob Kidd
Used with the permission of the photographer
bobkiddphotography.com

Poet in the Park and the *Solemn Swan* colophon are trademarks registered with the United States Patent and Trademark Offices.

The poems, images and design of this book were all created by Garrett Buhl Robinson.

Garrett Buhl Robinson © 2020
All Rights Reserved

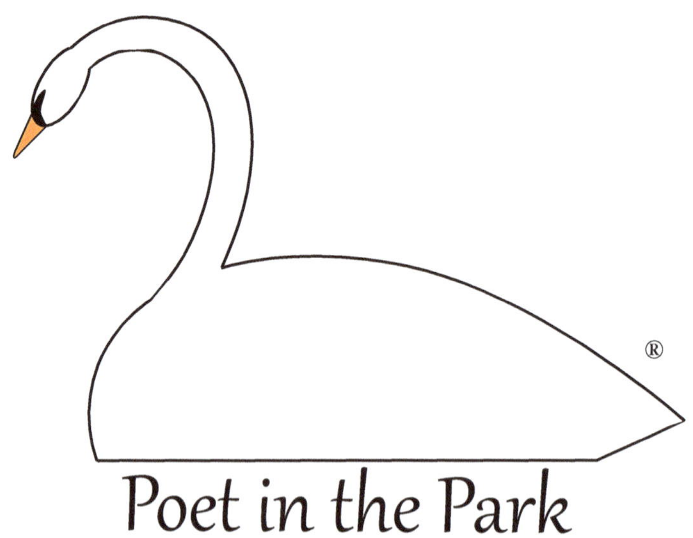

Poet in the Park
In Humanity I see Grace, Beauty and Dignity.

Poet in the Park.com

Table of Contents

The heart of this city is found in the lives of the residents
and in every visitor who has ever gazed up at the sunlight
glinting at the tips of these towers and raced through the
exhilarating pace of this tireless place.

This book is dedicated
to the People and the Poetry
of New York City.

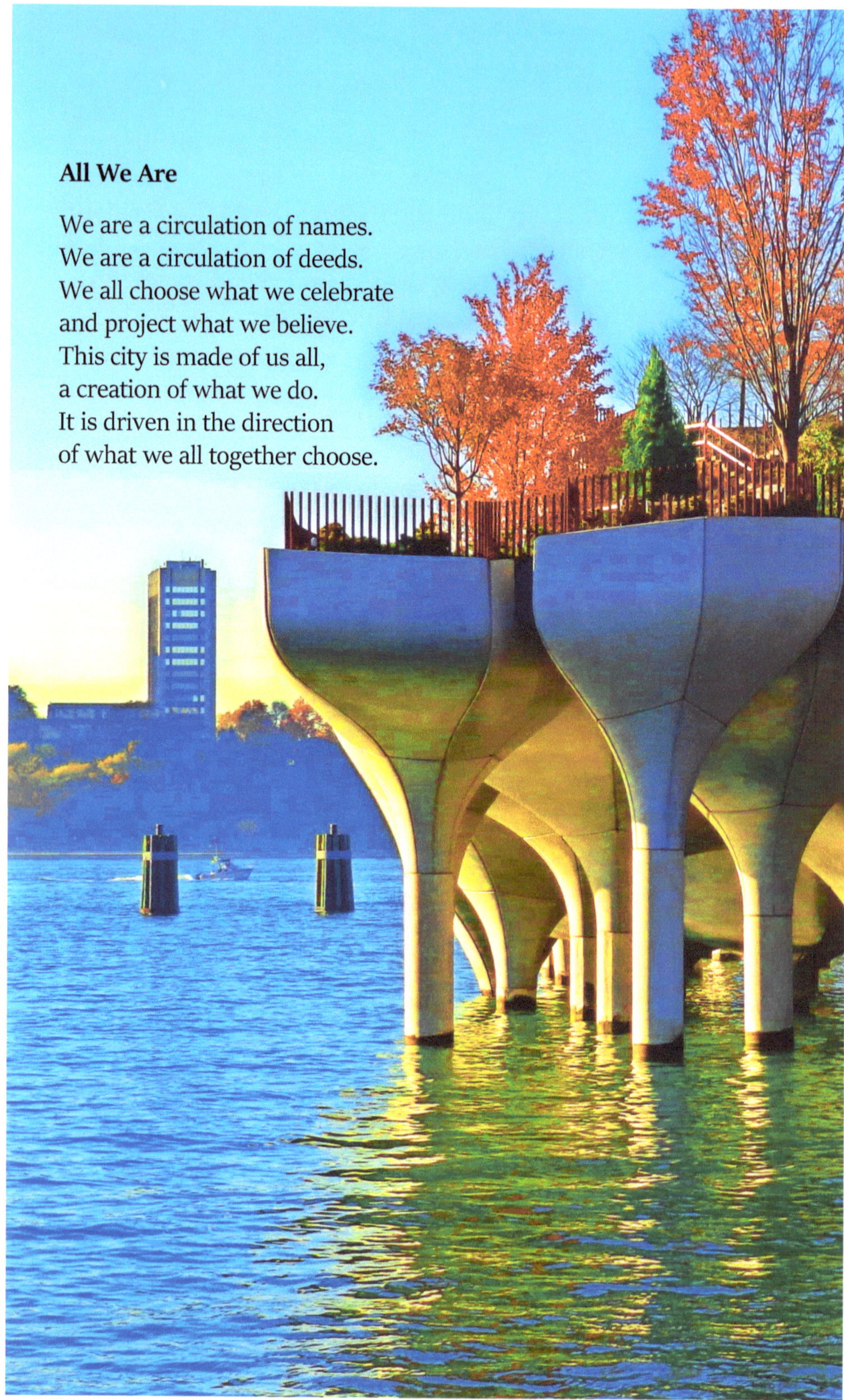

All We Are

We are a circulation of names.
We are a circulation of deeds.
We all choose what we celebrate
and project what we believe.
This city is made of us all,
a creation of what we do.
It is driven in the direction
of what we all together choose.

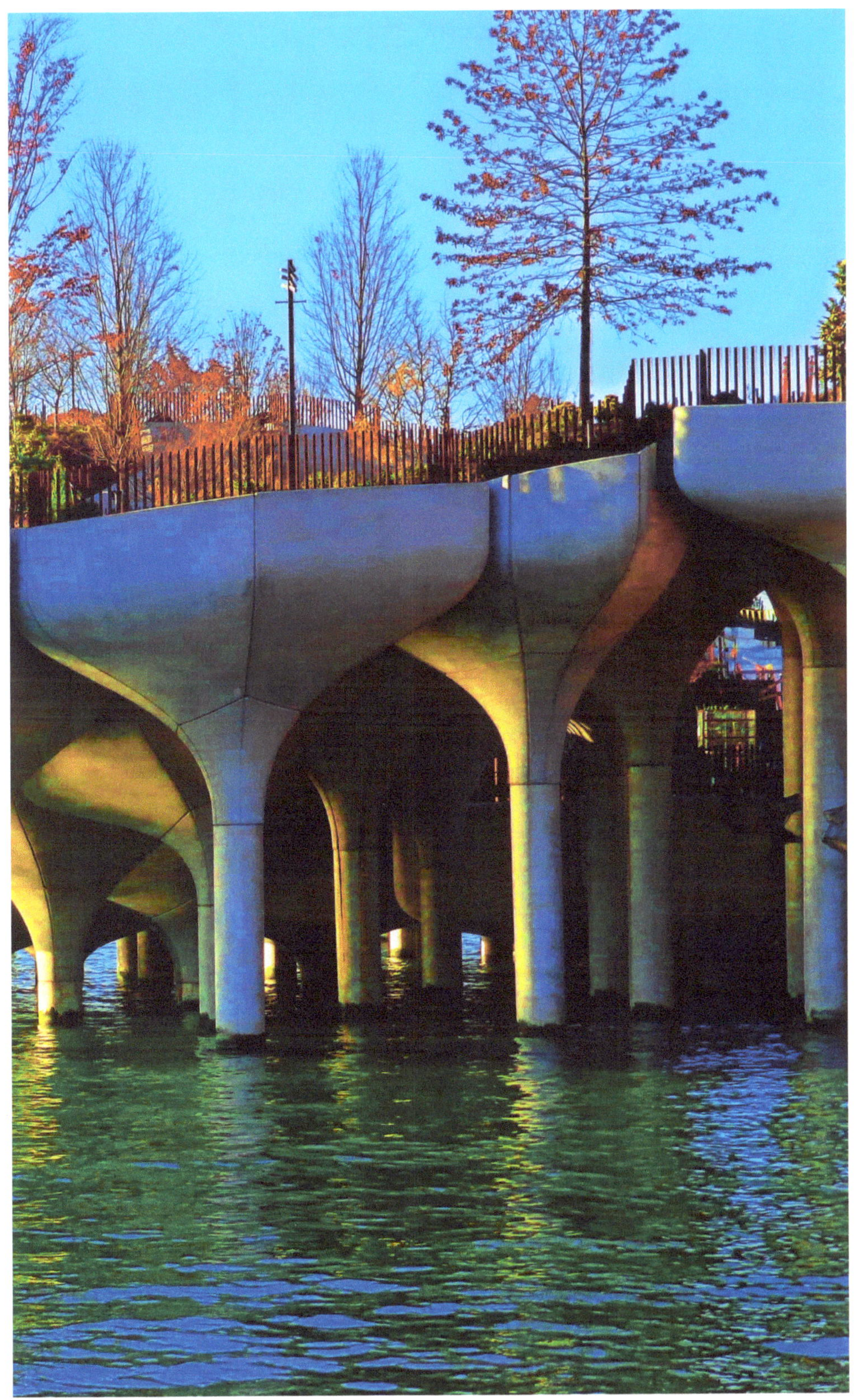

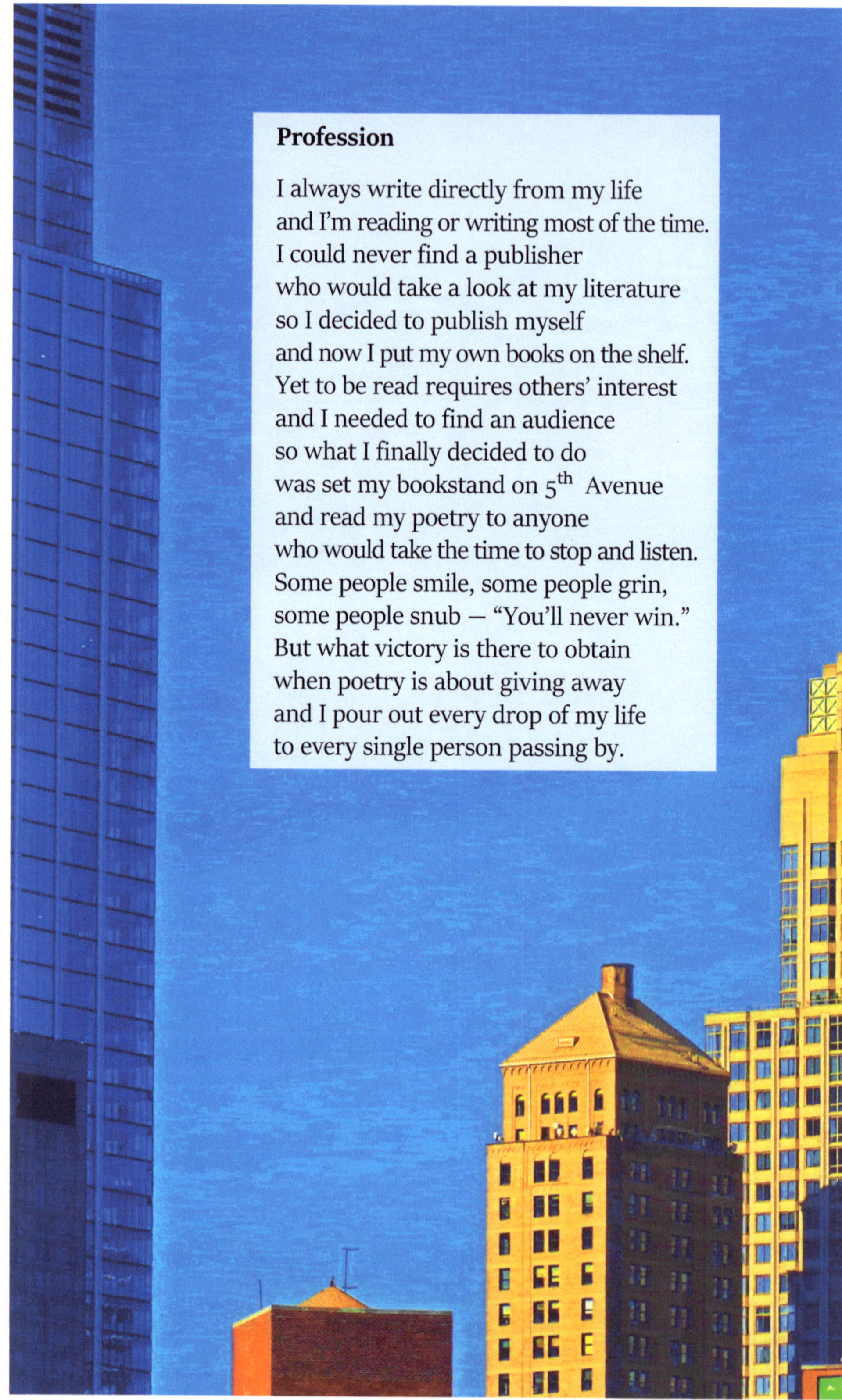

Profession

I always write directly from my life
and I'm reading or writing most of the time.
I could never find a publisher
who would take a look at my literature
so I decided to publish myself
and now I put my own books on the shelf.
Yet to be read requires others' interest
and I needed to find an audience
so what I finally decided to do
was set my bookstand on 5th Avenue
and read my poetry to anyone
who would take the time to stop and listen.
Some people smile, some people grin,
some people snub — "You'll never win."
But what victory is there to obtain
when poetry is about giving away
and I pour out every drop of my life
to every single person passing by.

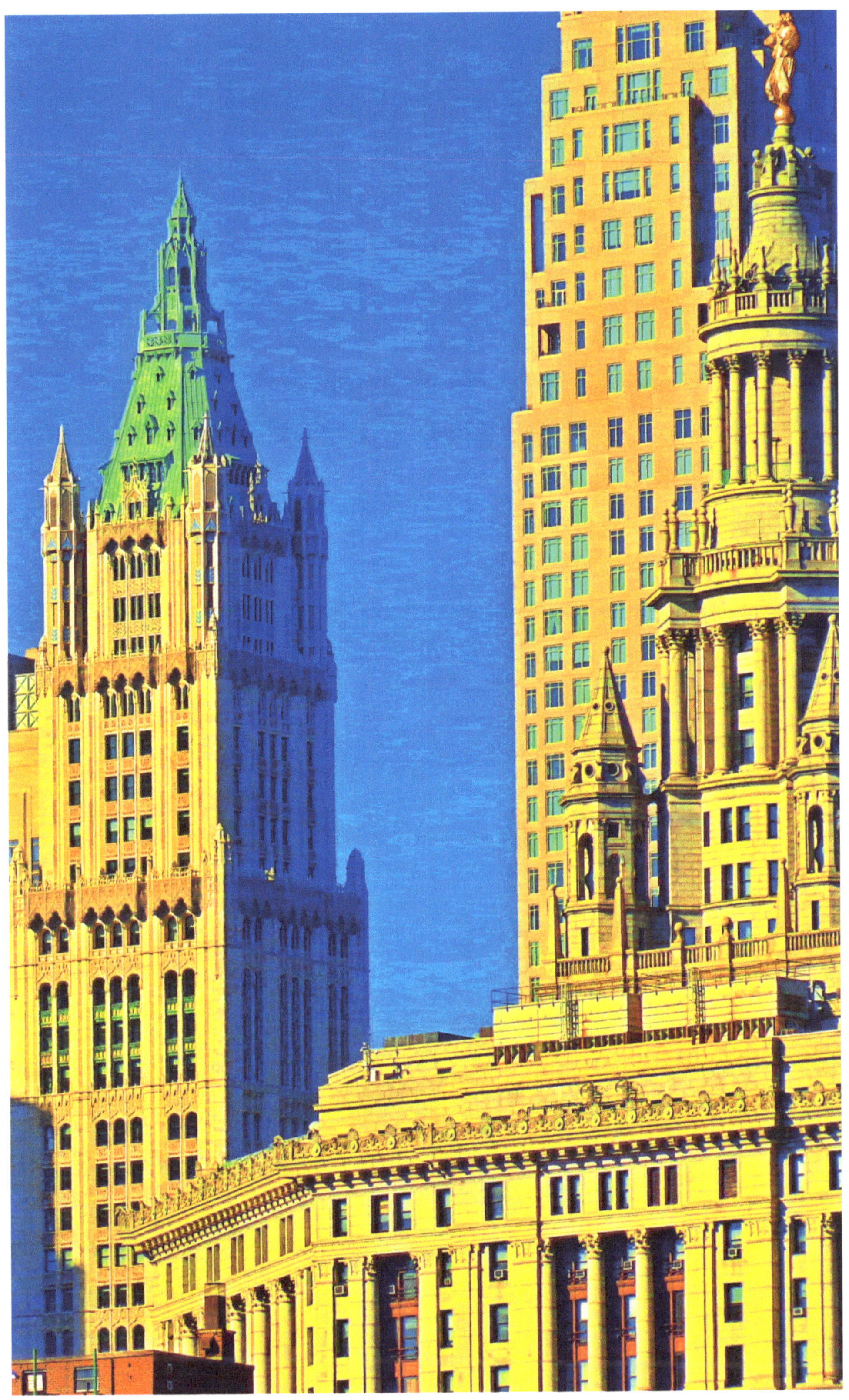

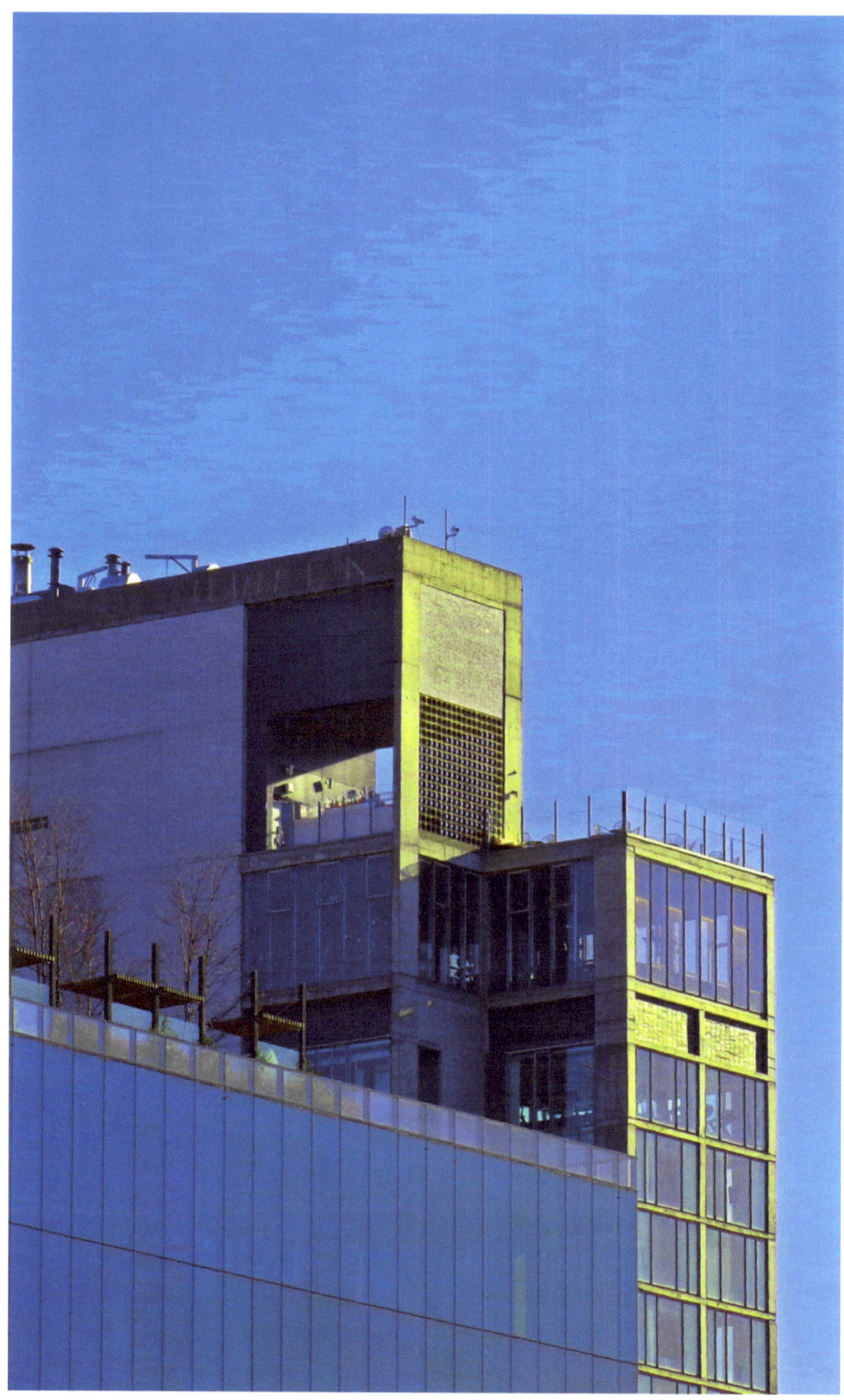

Blank Page

I labored over my lengthy notes
in hopes of finding a melodic ring
and in the stressed silence of what I wrote
a virtuosic bird began to sing.

I pondered on a maze inside my head
and no longer knew what I was moving toward
and I recalled something Merce Cunningham said,
"The direction you are facing is forward."

I was lost and staggering through the night
with everything obstructed from my view
then the world was drawn on a thread of moonlight
reflected on a gathered drop of dew.

Complexity can be very obtuse,
overworking can blur the clarity,
too many choices make it tough to choose
and abandons me in obscurity.

When I am distressed it is tough to relax,
though it would seem the easiest thing to do
but I've always found this ironic fact —
the obvious is often obscured from view.

Trying to Understand What's Overlooked

We all reach out and all in our own way
we're all vexed at times we are turned away.
Perhaps I offer what no one can accept,
perhaps I offer what causes others offense
but my reach is never to grab or punch
I simply and tenderly extend a touch
with presents of my meager offerings —
sometimes a poem inscribed on my palm,
sometimes the opening of a new song
that might flutter up on delightful wings.
Maybe I'm only winnowing away
but in the drifting chaff there are some grains
that the gleaners will always overlook
and scarcely and sparingly they take root
to flower and bear sweet burdens of fruit.

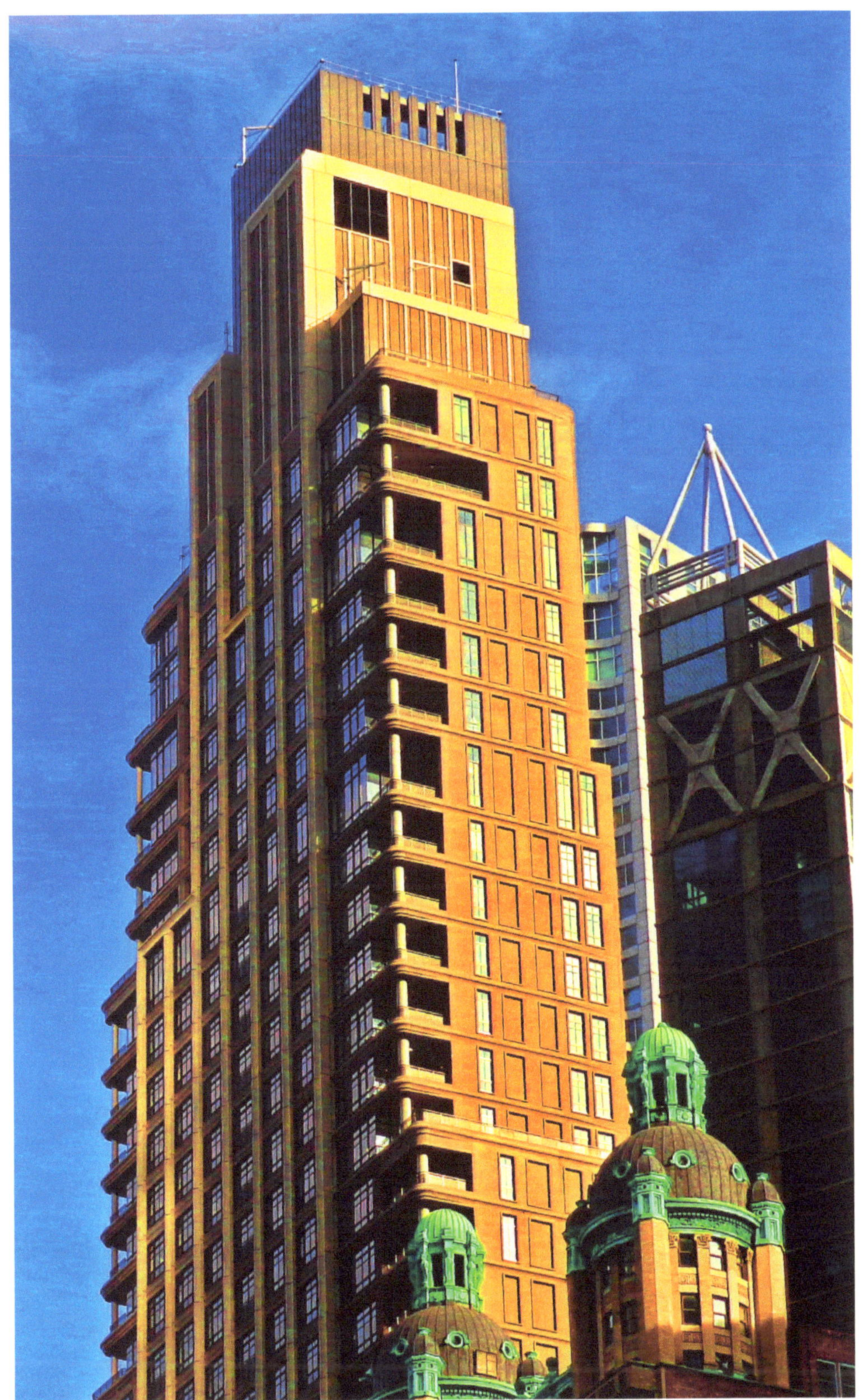

City River

There is so little I can control.
The water is always up to my chin
and this cold river could swallow me whole.

Sometimes I feel my life is not my own.
Nothing ever develops as I intend.
There is so little I can control.

All I can do is try to stay afloat.
No time for what will be or what has been.
This roaring river could swallow me whole.

Most often I must simply go with the flow.
It's futile to fight this current I'm in.
There is so little I can control.

Where we're going, nobody knows
and the more we struggle the more we descend
and this relentless river could swallow us whole.

I have my focus and attention though
and in what I love is in what I live.
This is all I can hope to control
else this river would swallow me whole.

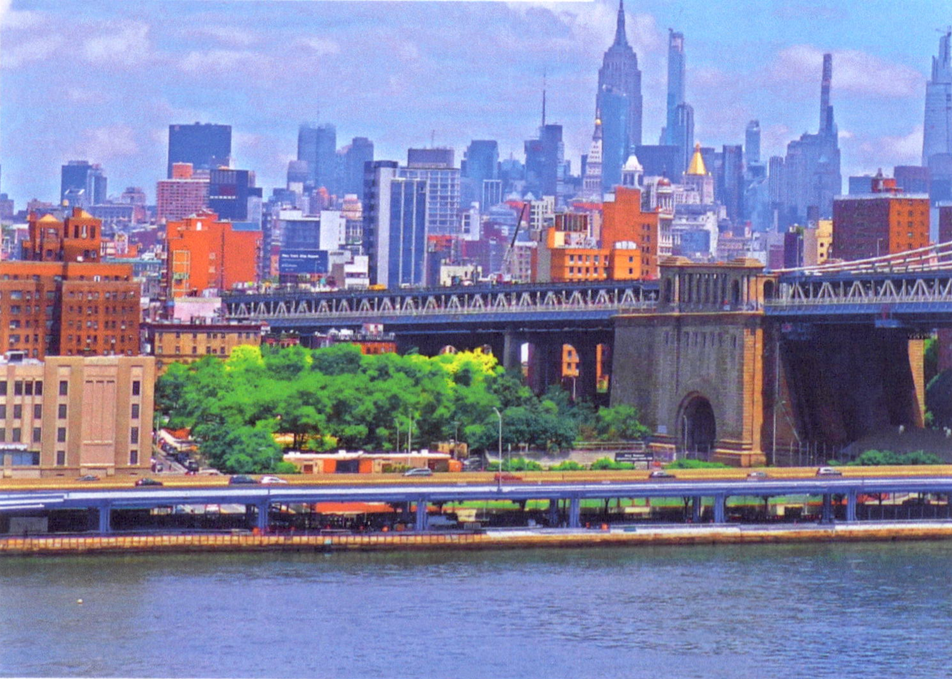

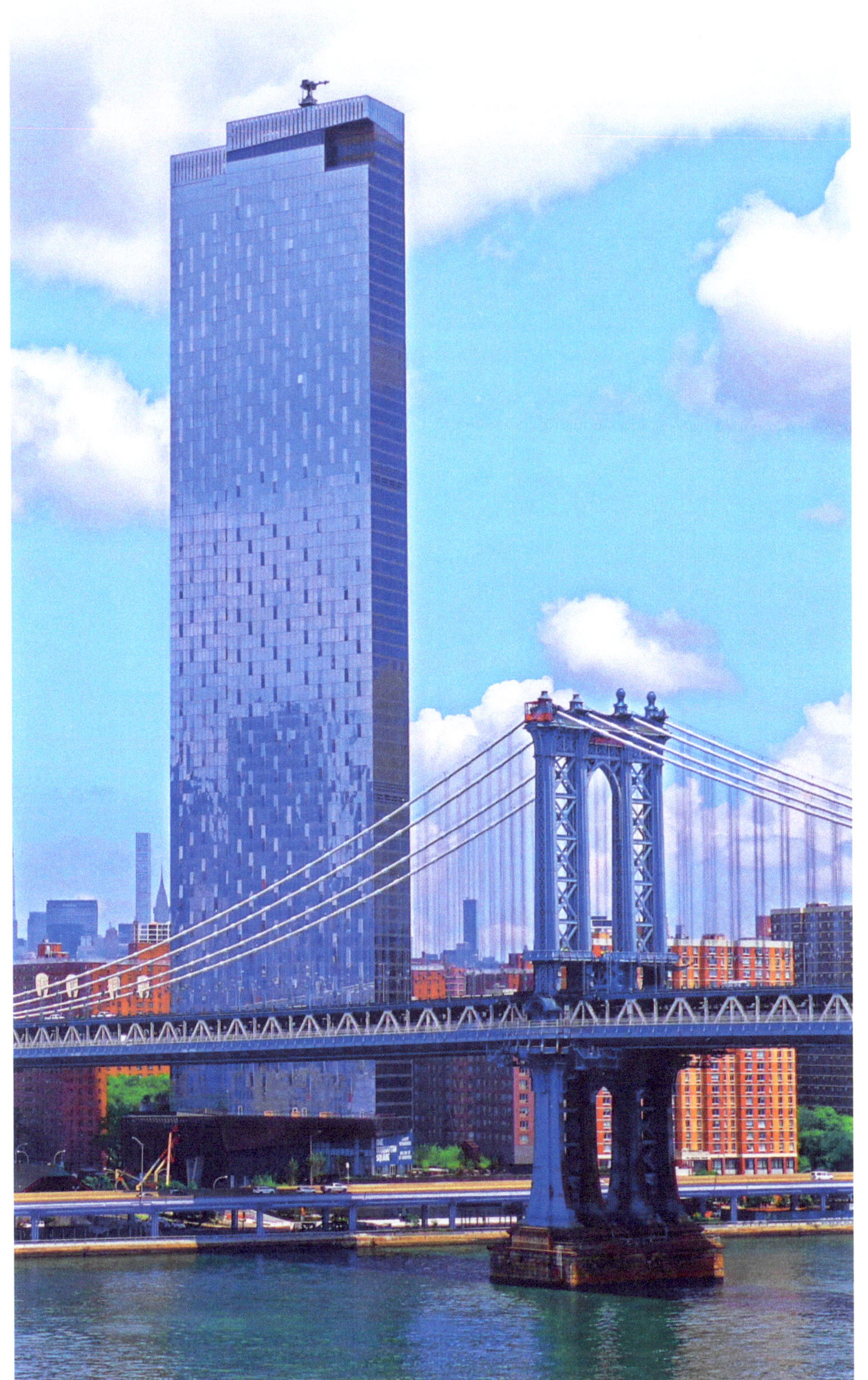

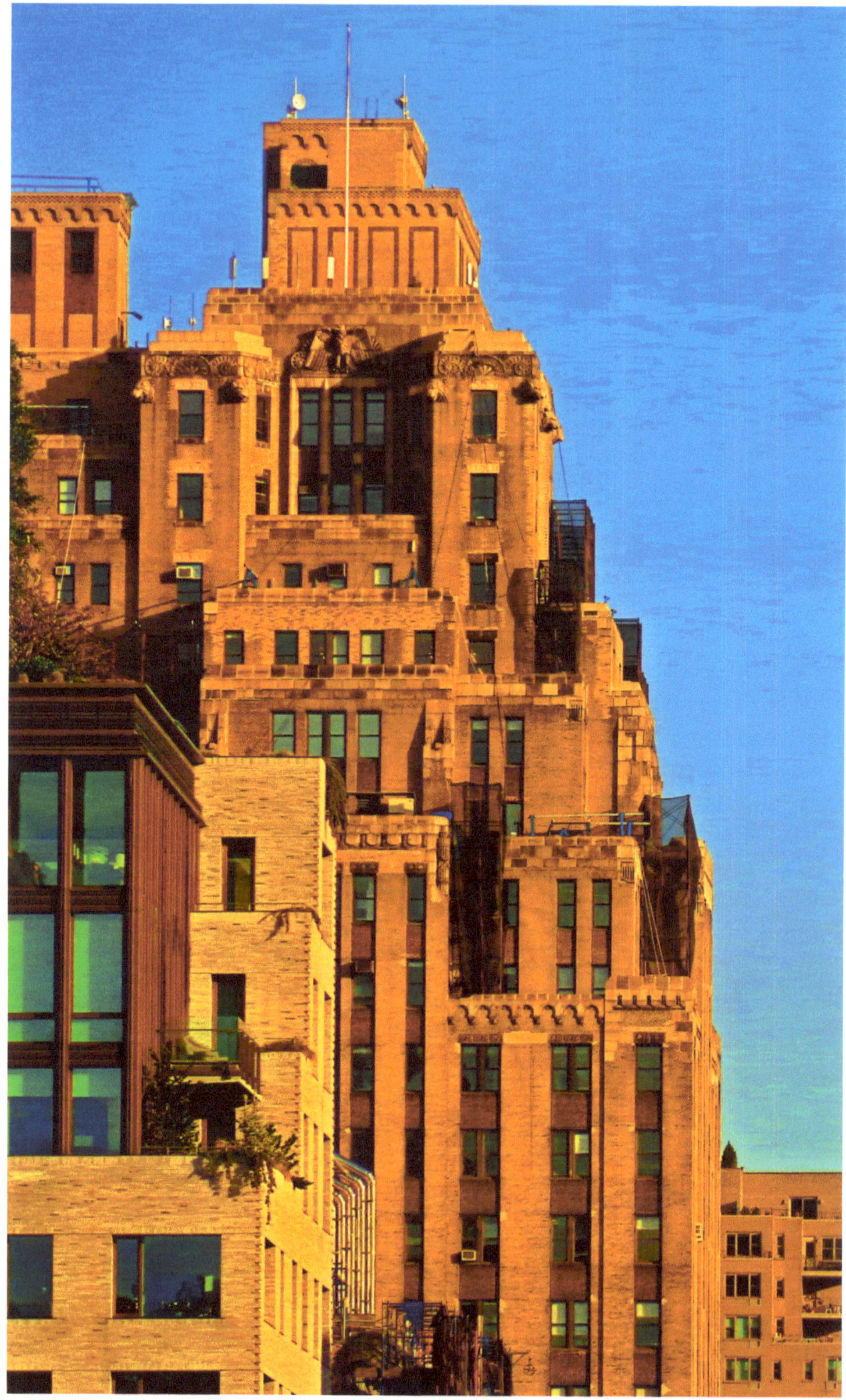

Insubstantial Things

This little machine is made out of sounds,
phenomenal waves bouncing around.
There are little springs made of surprises,
tightening suspense before unwinding.
The teeth of the gears are turning phrases
incremental syntactical arrangements
opening curious whimsical doors
into the most fantastic corridors
that are illuminated with intrigue
and completely filled with discovery.
All this is built upon structural beams
mined and refined from what it seems to mean
and furnished with what anyone believes
who cares to venture into this sweet dream
that is not exactly particular
but absolutely peculiar.

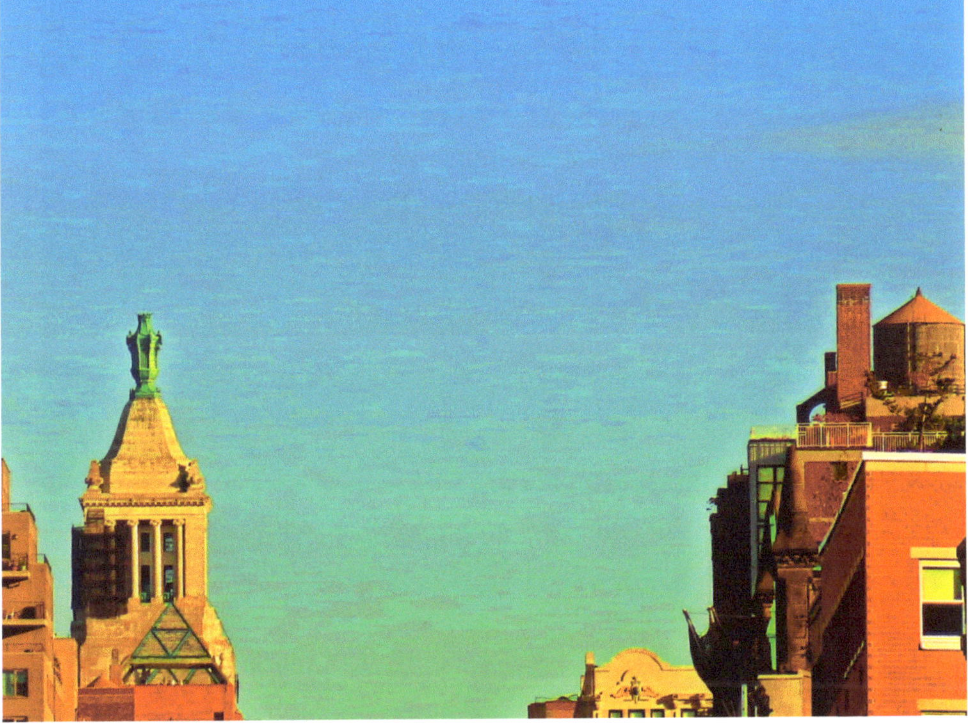

Then extending out in every direction
through each and every conceivable connection
intersecting and projecting this design
designates its specific place in time
by simply realizing its own presence
as the assurance of its relevance.
After all, where it exists is its home
made up of possibilities alone,
a potential of pure space that is shaped
with the contours of an elegant vase
yet not burdened with any weight
and found in any and every place —
a little situated designation
perfect for endless contemplation.

The ones I know are in lyrical lines
and when the book is open they may rise
to swiftly dart and fly through glowing skies
of anyone's imaginative mind.
If some say they are empty, then I say
they are actually an opening
as I continue tinkering away
with my insubstantial things.

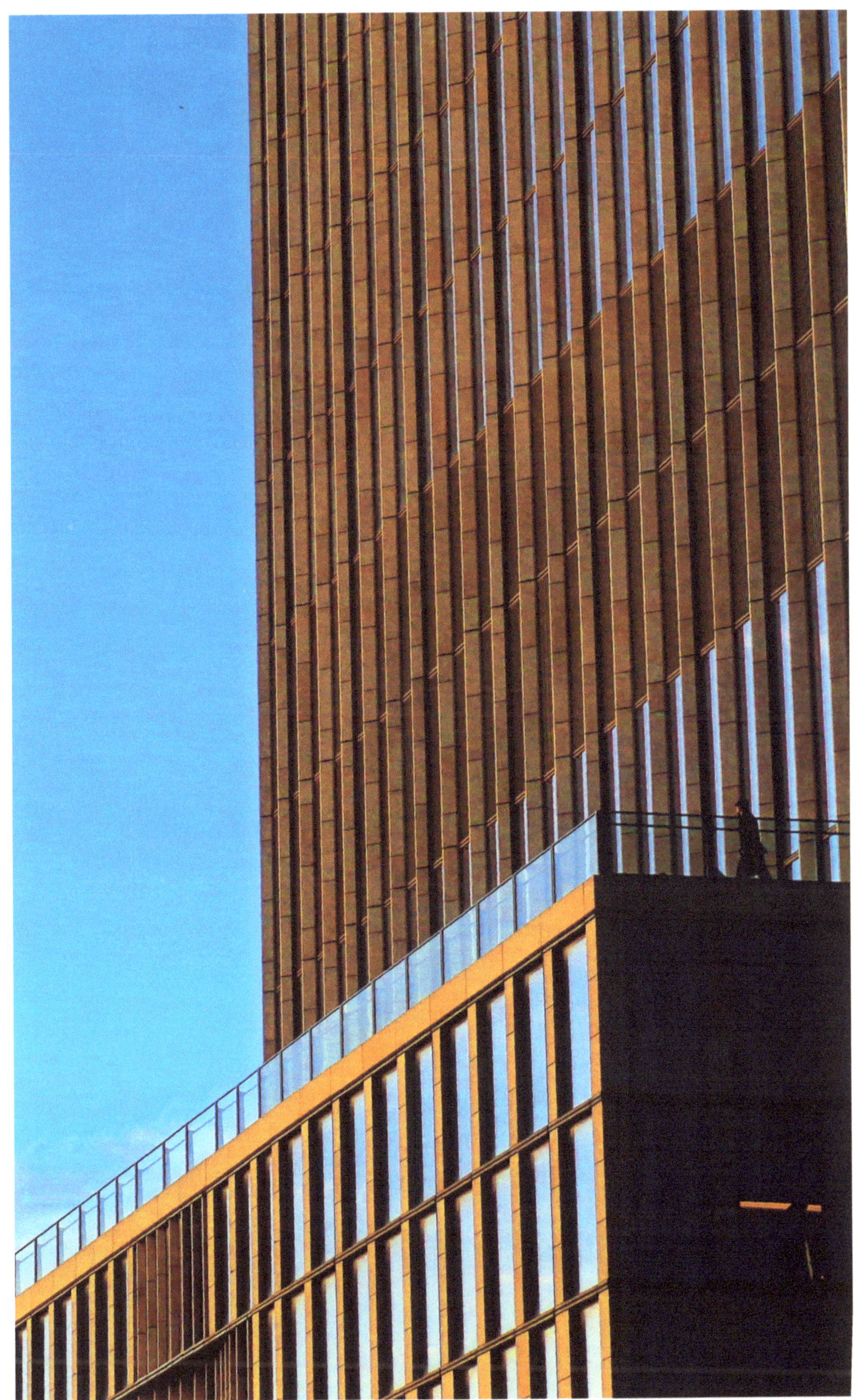

Beautiful Amusement

Some use the scholarly term aesthetics,
others may prefer to say enjoyment,
but there are a number of directions
for us to realize beauty's existence.

We may say it's what best befits our senses —
a metaphorical taste's appeasement
or perhaps a physical enrichment
with vital and substantial nourishment.
It may be a robust enlivenment
or an exploratory enticement.
There may even be some type of measure
to quantify and calculate pleasure
through how we feel we are best engaged
in the manner and means life is sustained
by finding the agreeable balance
between benefits and beneficence.

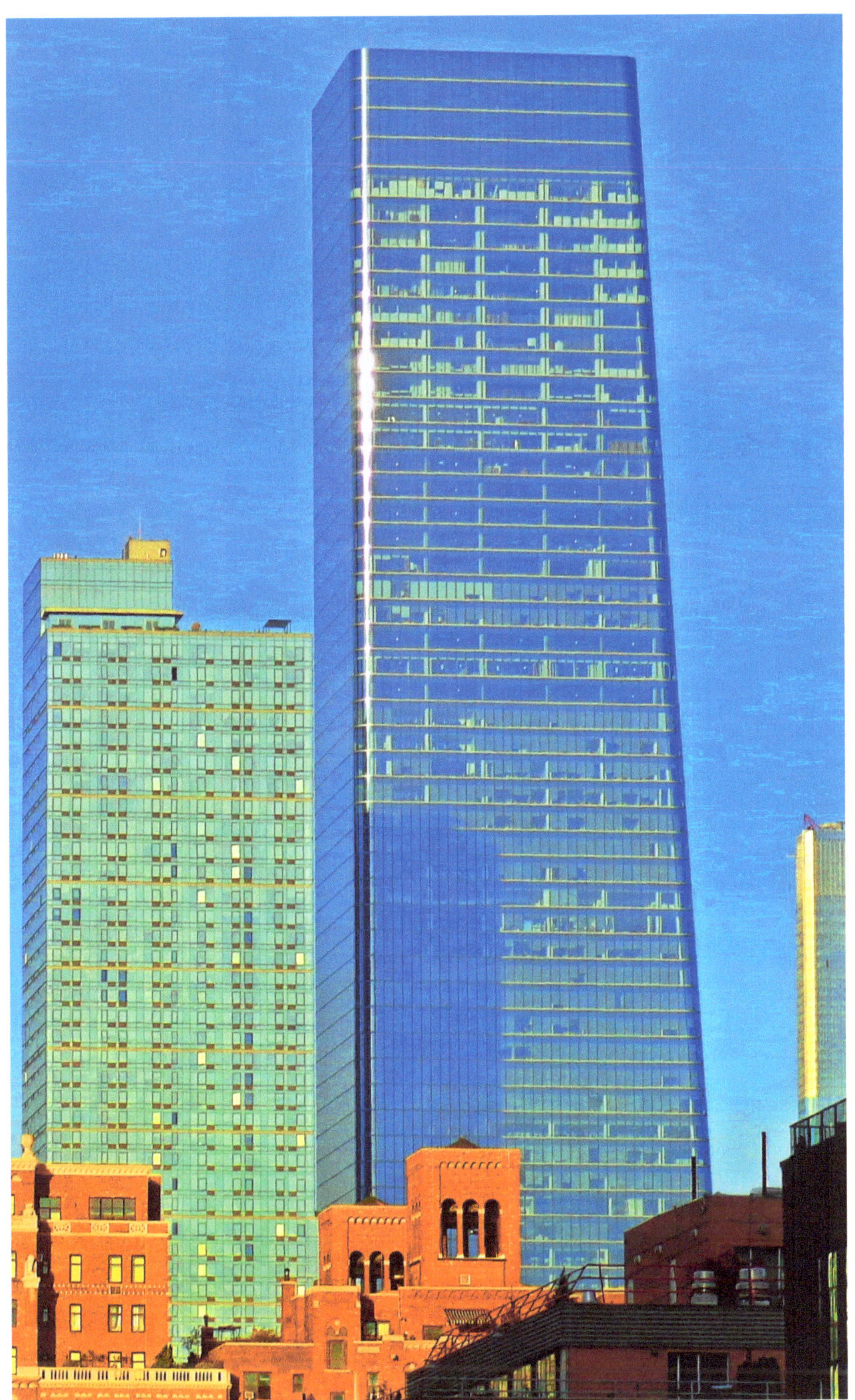

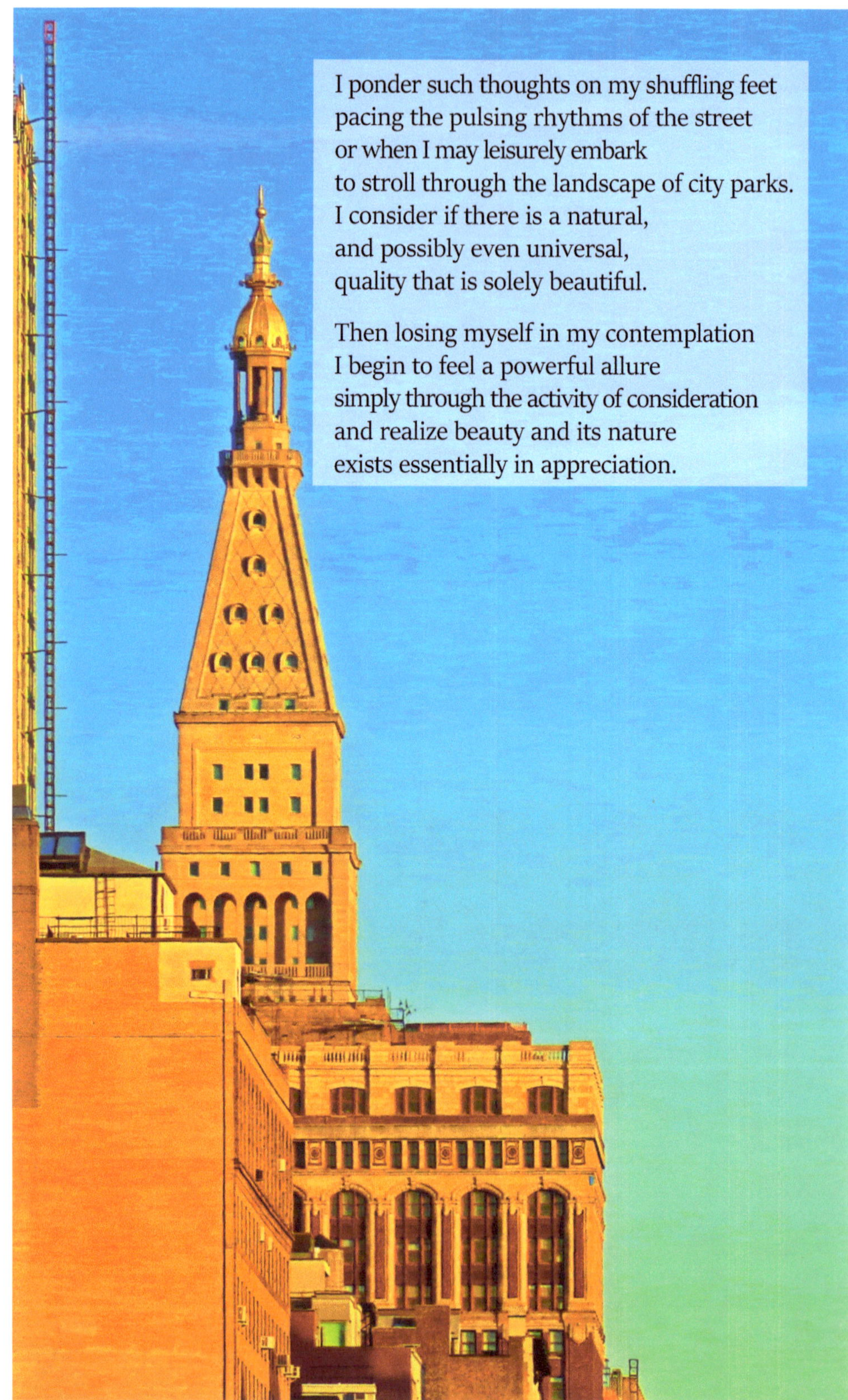

I ponder such thoughts on my shuffling feet
pacing the pulsing rhythms of the street
or when I may leisurely embark
to stroll through the landscape of city parks.
I consider if there is a natural,
and possibly even universal,
quality that is solely beautiful.

Then losing myself in my contemplation
I begin to feel a powerful allure
simply through the activity of consideration
and realize beauty and its nature
exists essentially in appreciation.

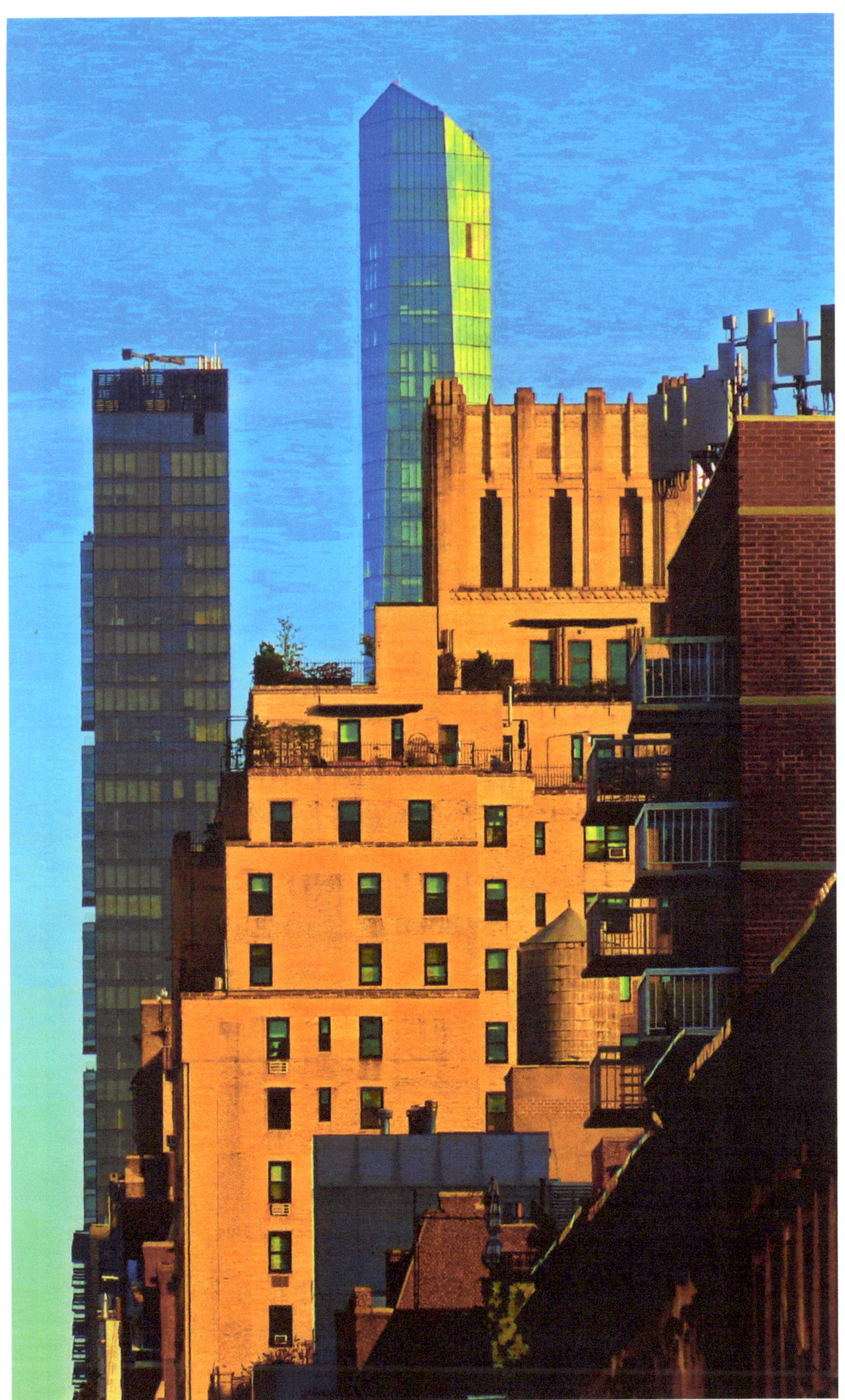

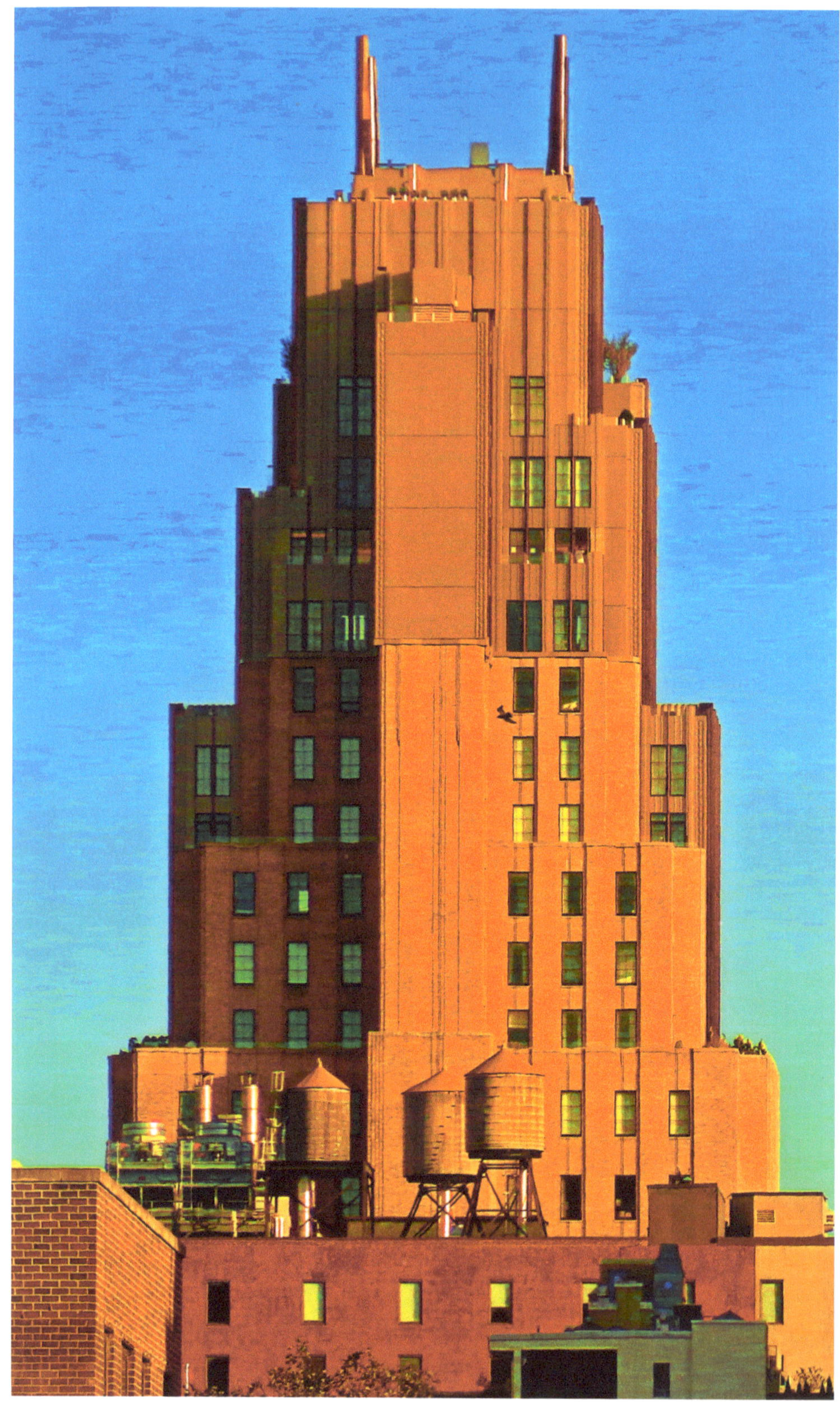

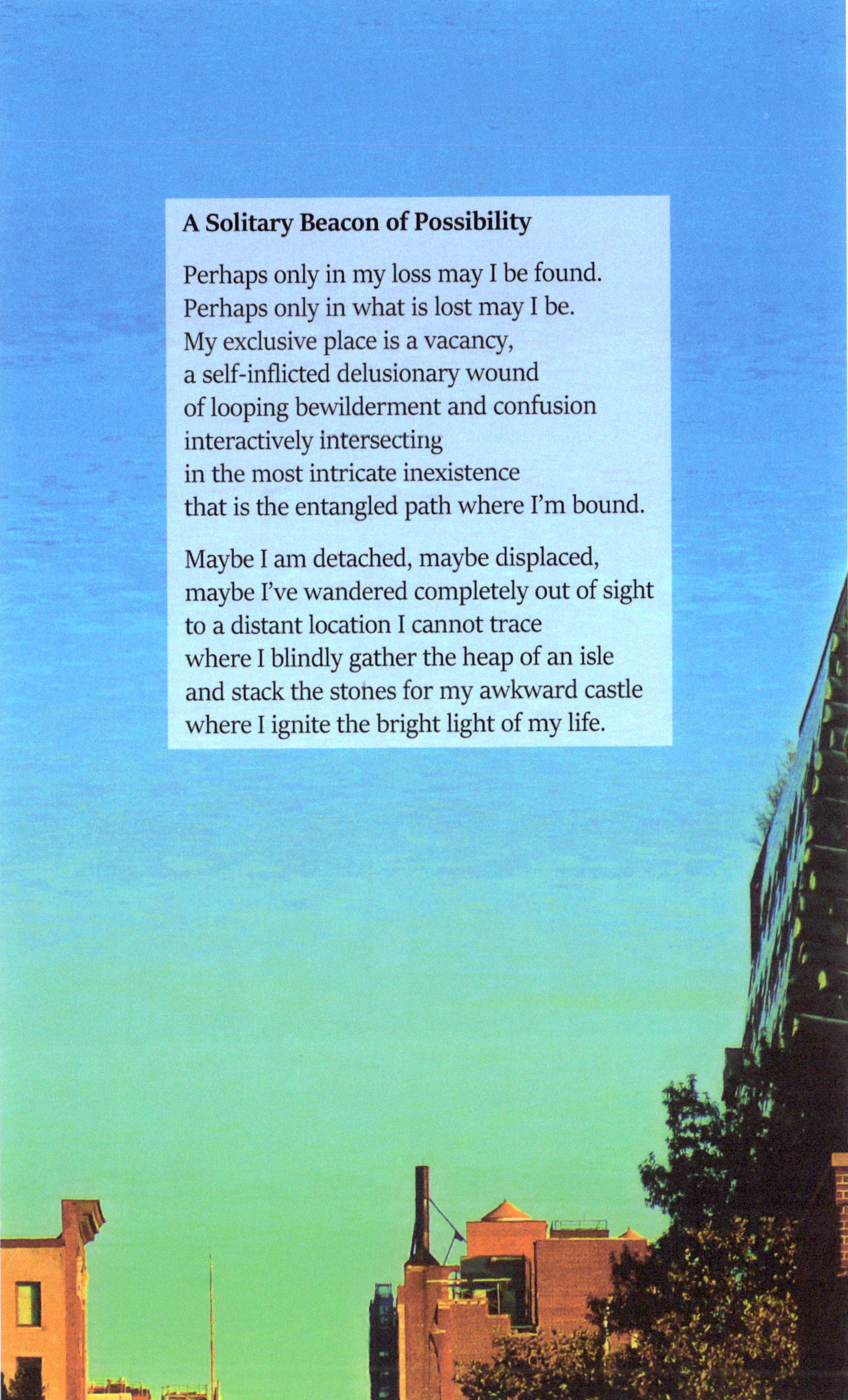

A Solitary Beacon of Possibility

Perhaps only in my loss may I be found.
Perhaps only in what is lost may I be.
My exclusive place is a vacancy,
a self-inflicted delusionary wound
of looping bewilderment and confusion
interactively intersecting
in the most intricate inexistence
that is the entangled path where I'm bound.

Maybe I am detached, maybe displaced,
maybe I've wandered completely out of sight
to a distant location I cannot trace
where I blindly gather the heap of an isle
and stack the stones for my awkward castle
where I ignite the bright light of my life.

Literary Figures

Arriving, my first nights in the city
were spent in what I later found to be
the very last flop house on the Bowery.

I bought a postcard of the Brooklyn Bridge
and mailed it to myself to establish
an address for a proof of residence.

Then I registered at the library
where titles are shelved like towering buildings
and found a book of Hart Crane's poetry.

Like never before, I found myself walking
down the cobbled streets he described, stepping
into the poem caressed with expressions.

The swinging sounds of jazz gushed from clubs,
pouring and cascading down the blocks
with flashy brass, high hats and massive chops.

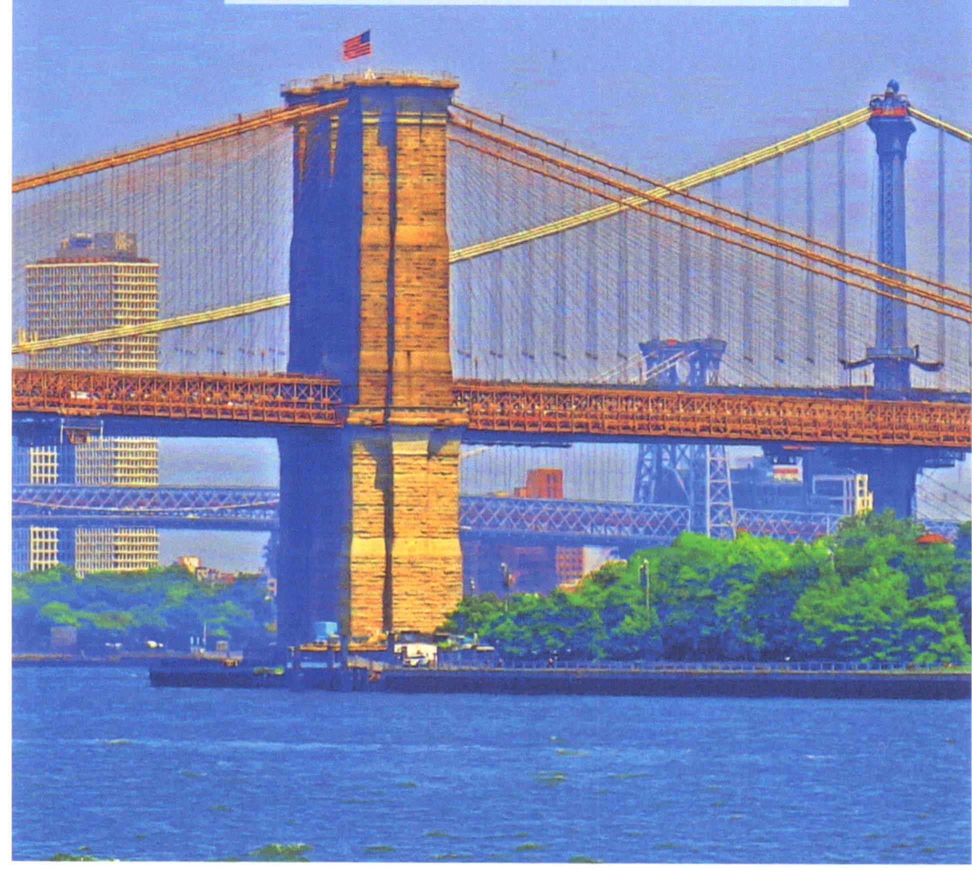

As I wandered deeper into the past,
I could hear Bartleby's muffled voice at last
and see Melville's bright eyes beautiful and sad.

I reached the East River eventually,
far from the deep of Rip Van Winkle's sleep
suddenly waking beneath the grinding

clock where crowds gathered at Times Square
to cheer the opening gate of another New Year.
Hart's poem still plays the city's music

as the vast operatic cast of Walt's *Leaves of Grass*
sing along staccato streets and allegro avenues
in a rapidly revolving and renewing mass.

Then with the surging tides swirling at their base,
I saw the bridge's towers standing in the current
and I saw Hart and Walt meet face to face.

The braided cable's tendon tension hums
as their hands clasp over the unraveling river
and they lift the city in their outstretched arms.

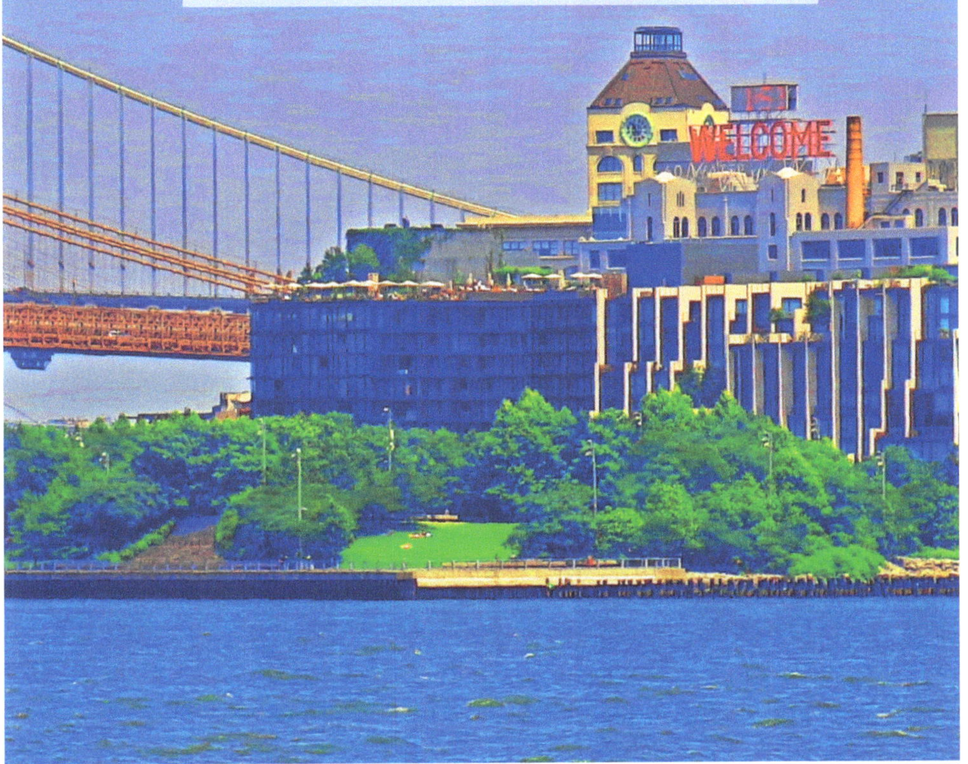

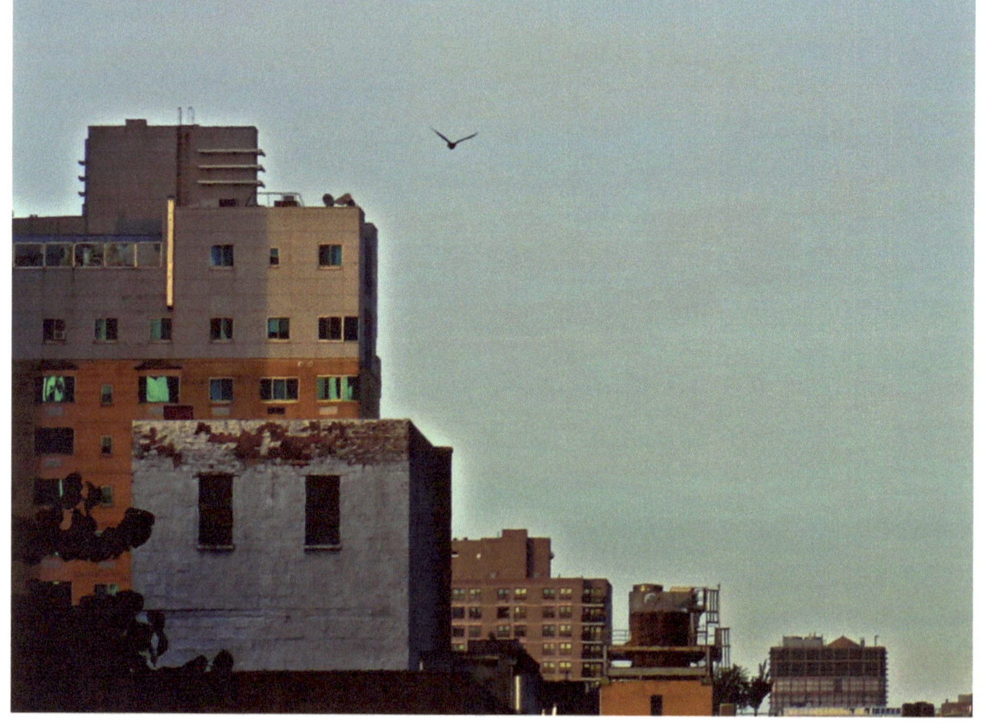

The Stuff of Dreams

Claiming there is more than what we can see,
the aim of a poet is an absurdity
relegated to a world of make believe
to champion fantastic reality.
Yet it is a matter of practicality
because when we hope to find a solution
in life's perplexing difficulties
our greatest tool is our imagination.
So let there be beauty and utility
with all the poets gathered together,
inspired to survive on the stuff of dreams,
depicting the mind in a world of letters,
drawing refreshment from a well of ink
and trying to fly with a single feather.

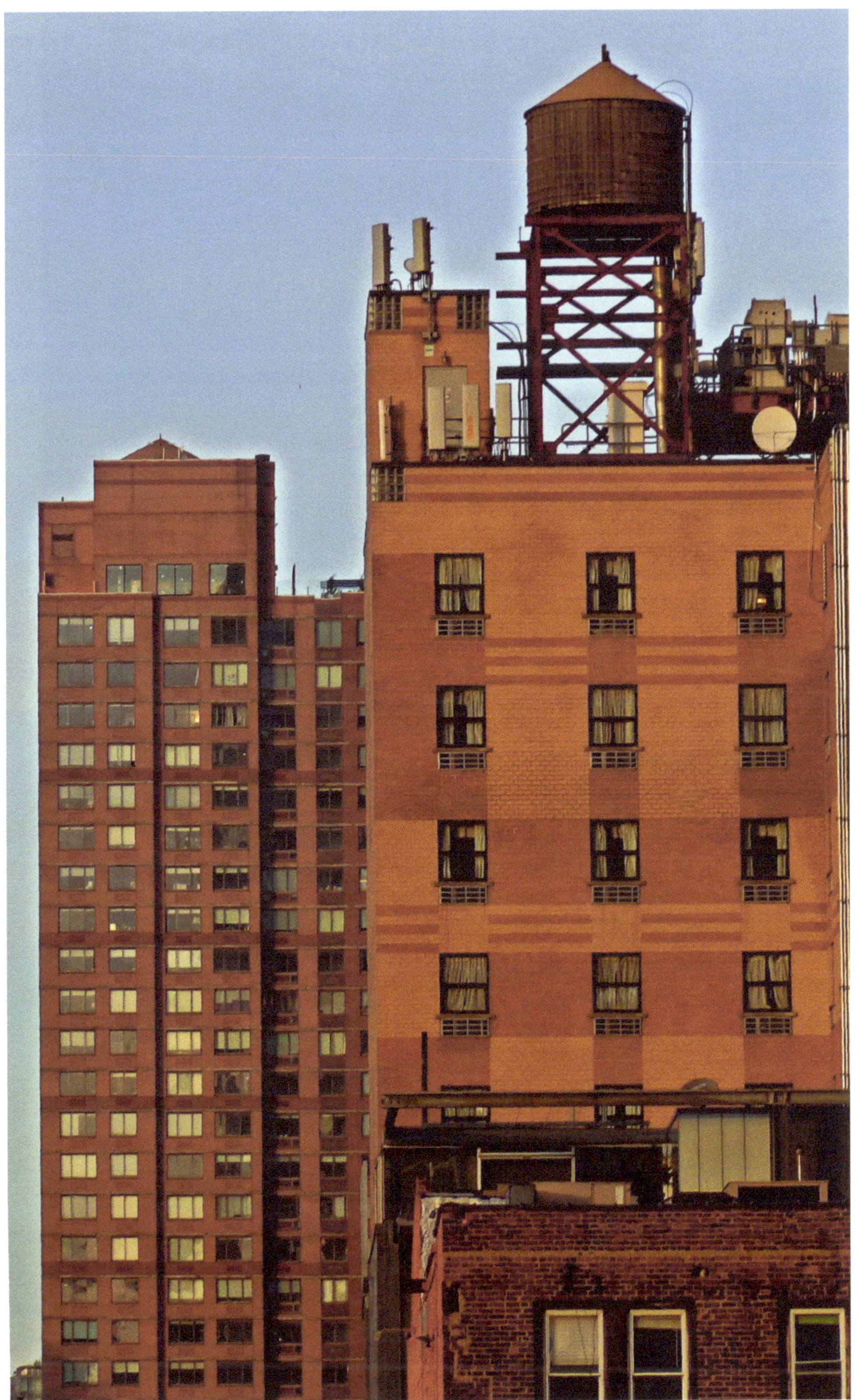

A Solemn Place

To be offered love — beautiful and true
and then walk away with nowhere to go,
what else could I be but a fool?

I've never known how to act or what to do
but she took me by the hand and led me home
and she gave me love — beautiful and true.

I didn't leave in search of something new.
I've simply learned to accept living alone.
What else could I be but a fool?

I understand I've always been confused
because confusion is all I've ever known
but she offered me love — beautiful and true.

I heard her call when I was out of view
but I turned from her warmth and back to my cold.
What else could I be but a fool?

I left before the Spring could ever bloom
and returned to my land of abandon.
I walked away from her love sweet and true.
What else could I be but a fool?

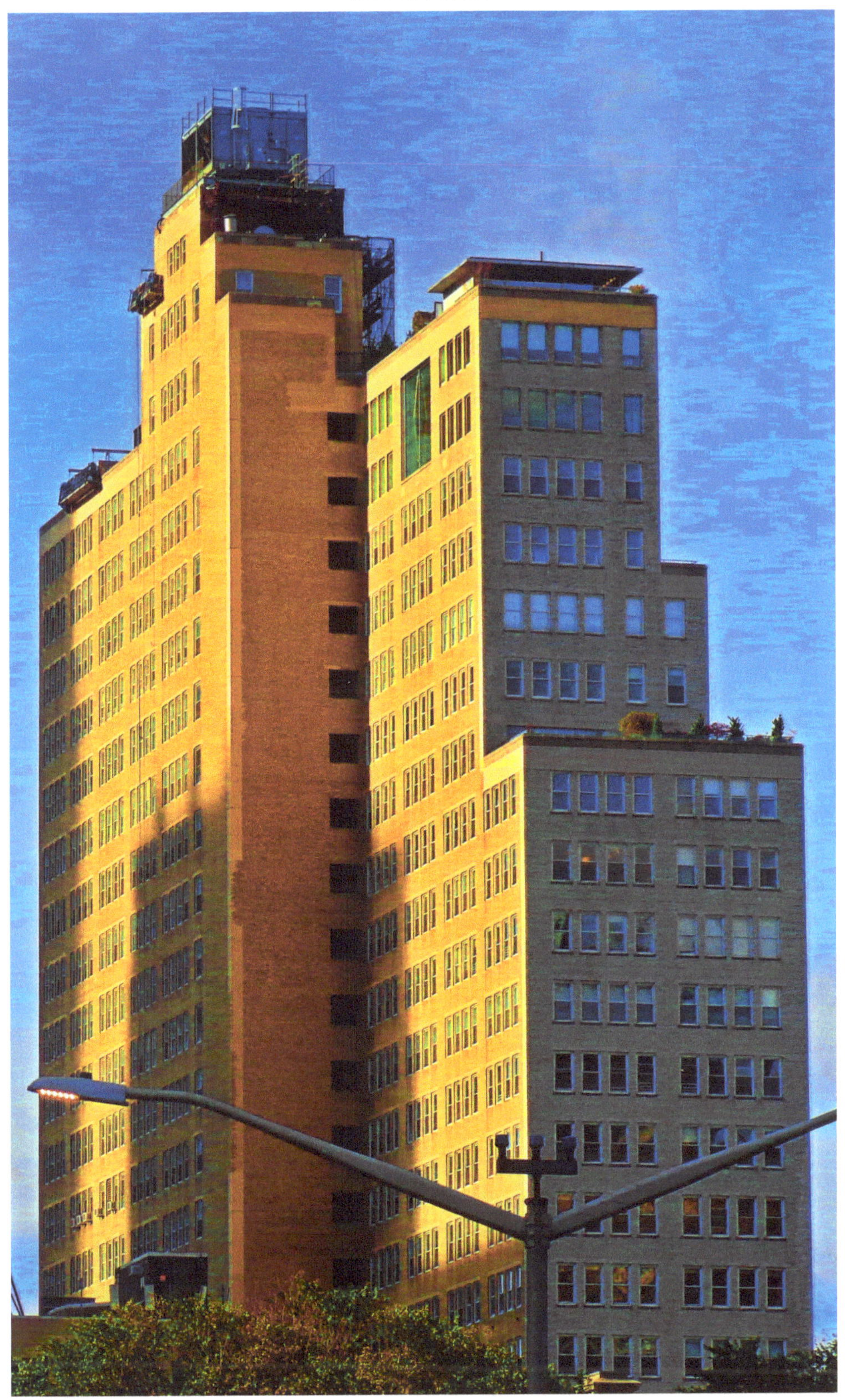

Echolocation

There are endless directions in life
but the one I unknowingly chose
is on an outstretching lyrical line
that spins out of the music I compose.
I take note of each and every step.
The key is to play even when practicing.
I steadily move, even through the rests,
in a realm that is imaginary.
Sometime the story of my song will close
and I suppose that will be my end
but for now I will continue to stroll
along a vocal chord tuned with the wind,
attached to an indistinct memory
and extending into a mystery.

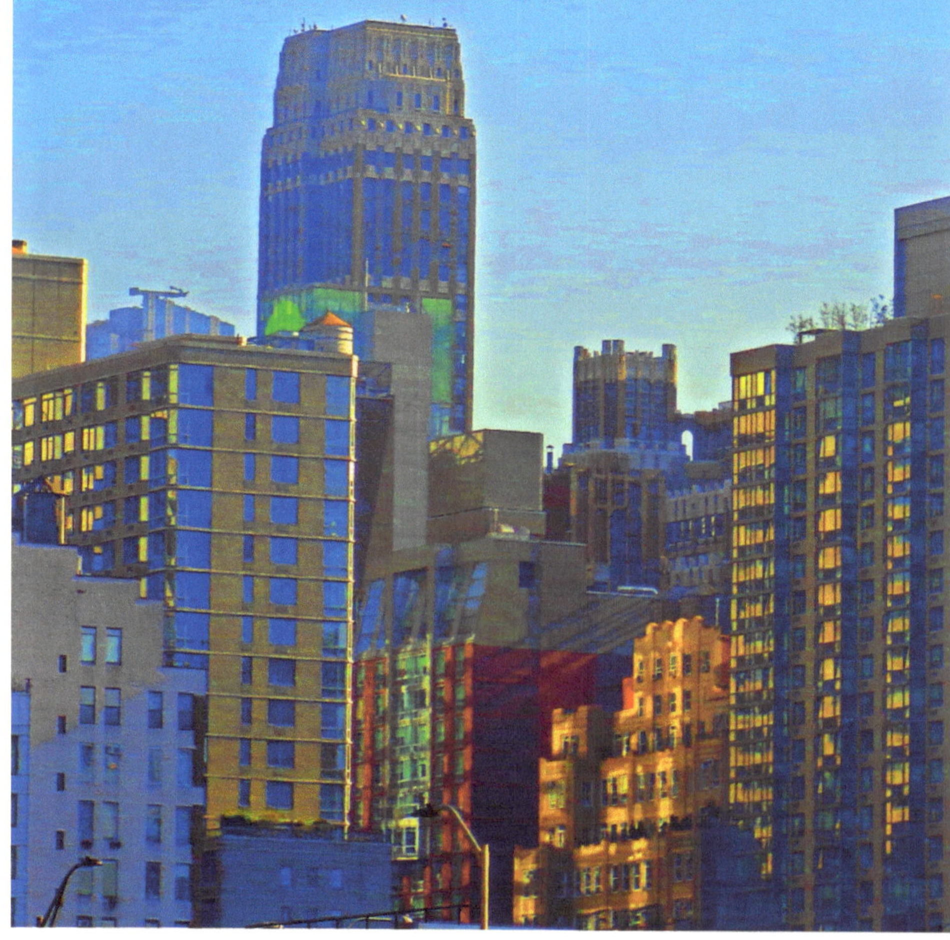

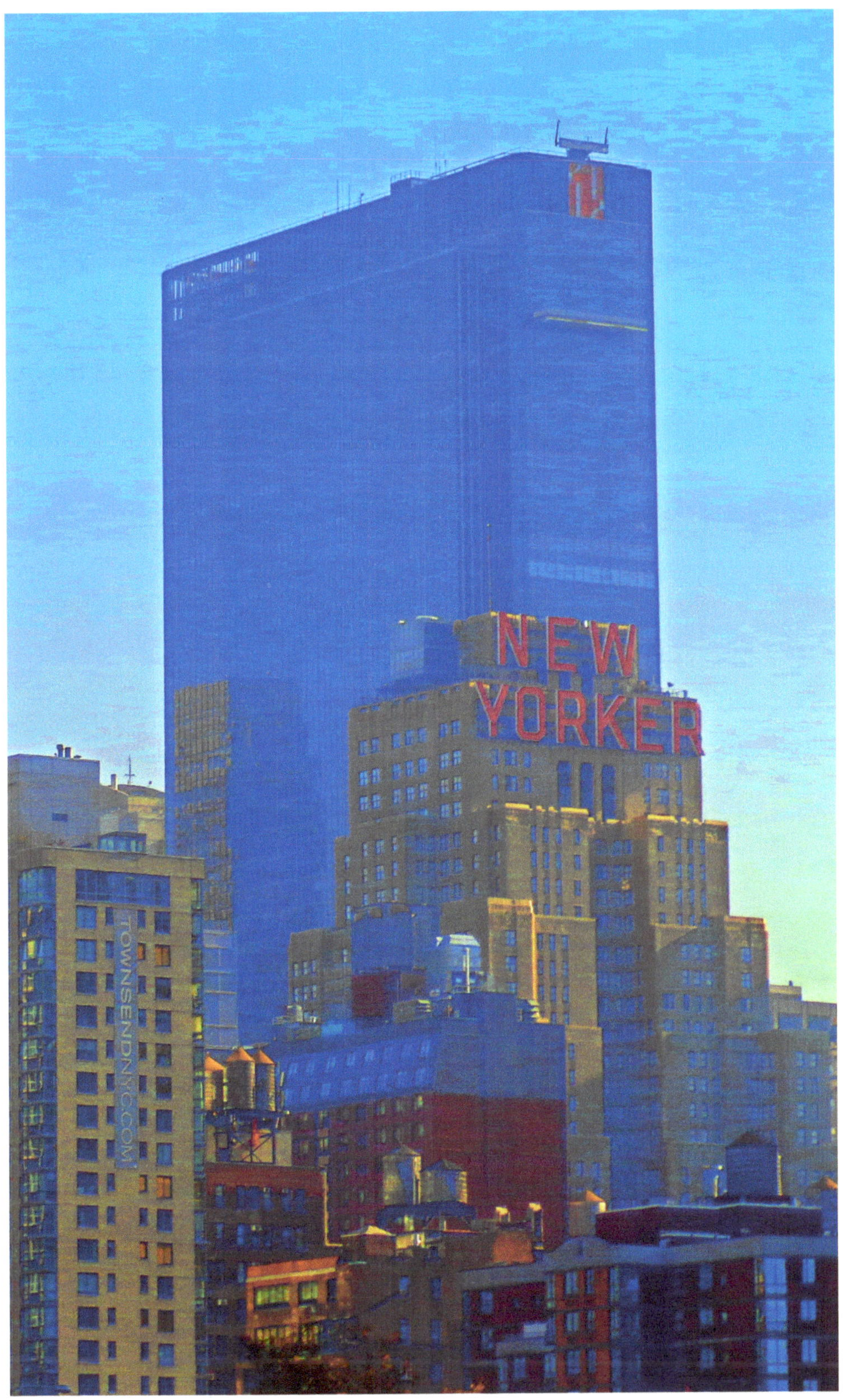
NEW
YORKER
TOWNSENDNYC.COM

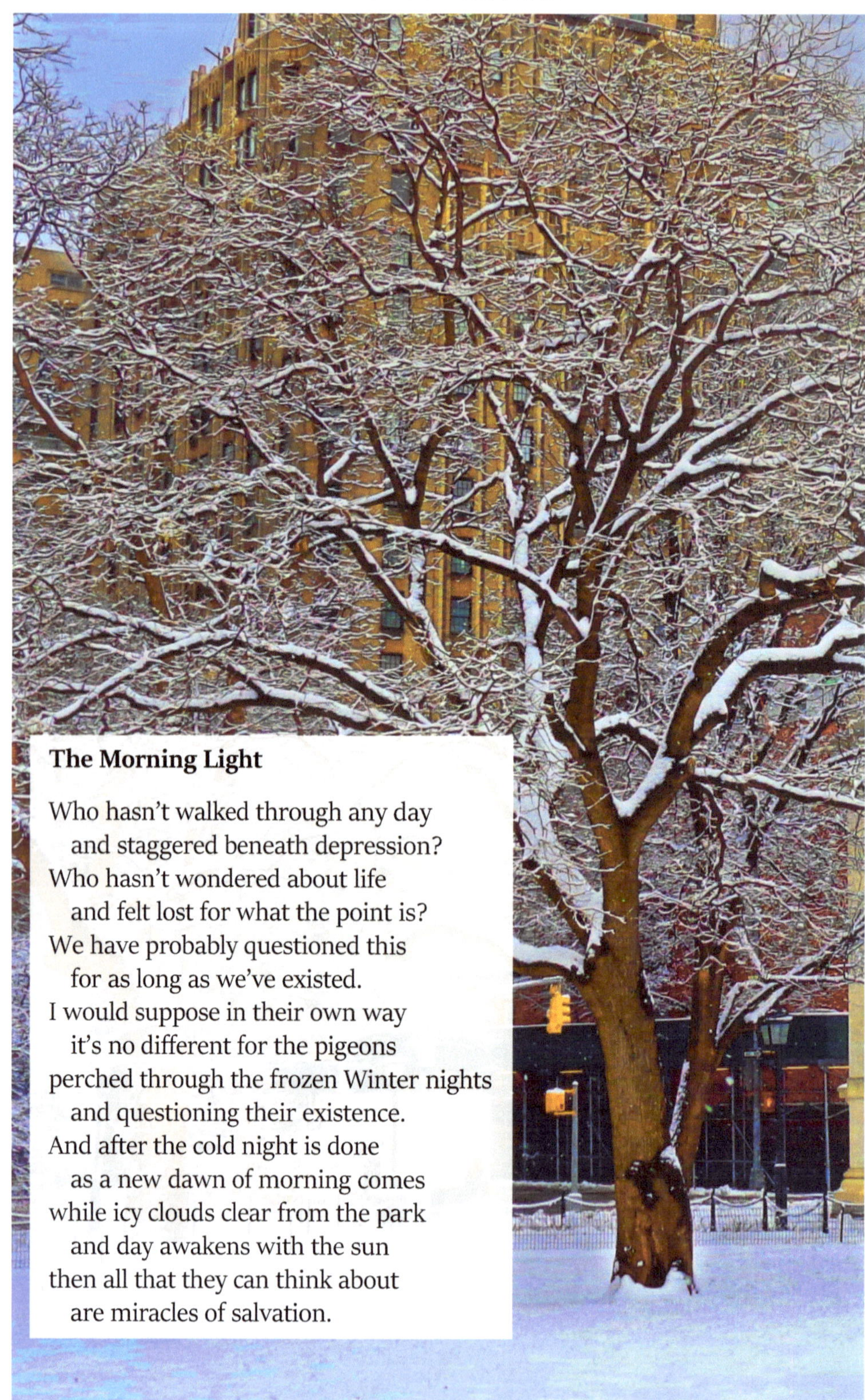

The Morning Light

Who hasn't walked through any day
    and staggered beneath depression?
Who hasn't wondered about life
    and felt lost for what the point is?
We have probably questioned this
    for as long as we've existed.
I would suppose in their own way
    it's no different for the pigeons
perched through the frozen Winter nights
    and questioning their existence.
And after the cold night is done
    as a new dawn of morning comes
while icy clouds clear from the park
    and day awakens with the sun
then all that they can think about
    are miracles of salvation.

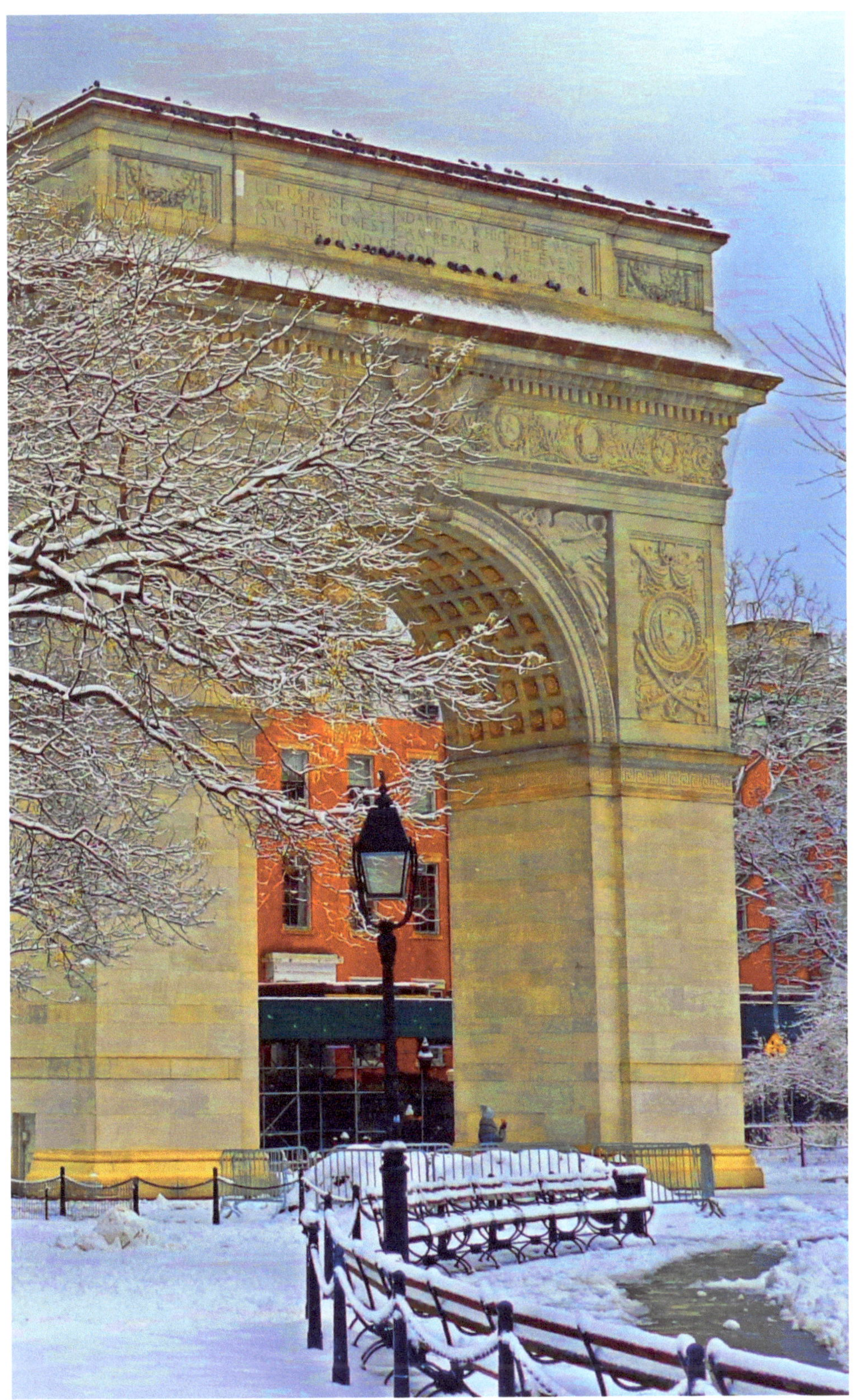

LET US RAISE A STANDARD TO WHICH THE WISE
AND THE HONEST CAN REPAIR THE EVENT
IS IN THE HAND OF GOD

Incidental Existence

I've known the Winters, we have known them all,
when the creaking limbs are stripped bare of leaves
that before had been singing in the breeze
then warmed our thoughts in the colorful Fall.
I have sunk with sap in the frozen ground
clenched with the roots of the outstanding trees,
yet buried deep beneath the scattered leaves
packed with the snow of the sky falling down
I remain a part of this bustling town.
The birds will certainly return to sing
and there will always be plenty more Springs
that turn into Summer's sweet offerings.

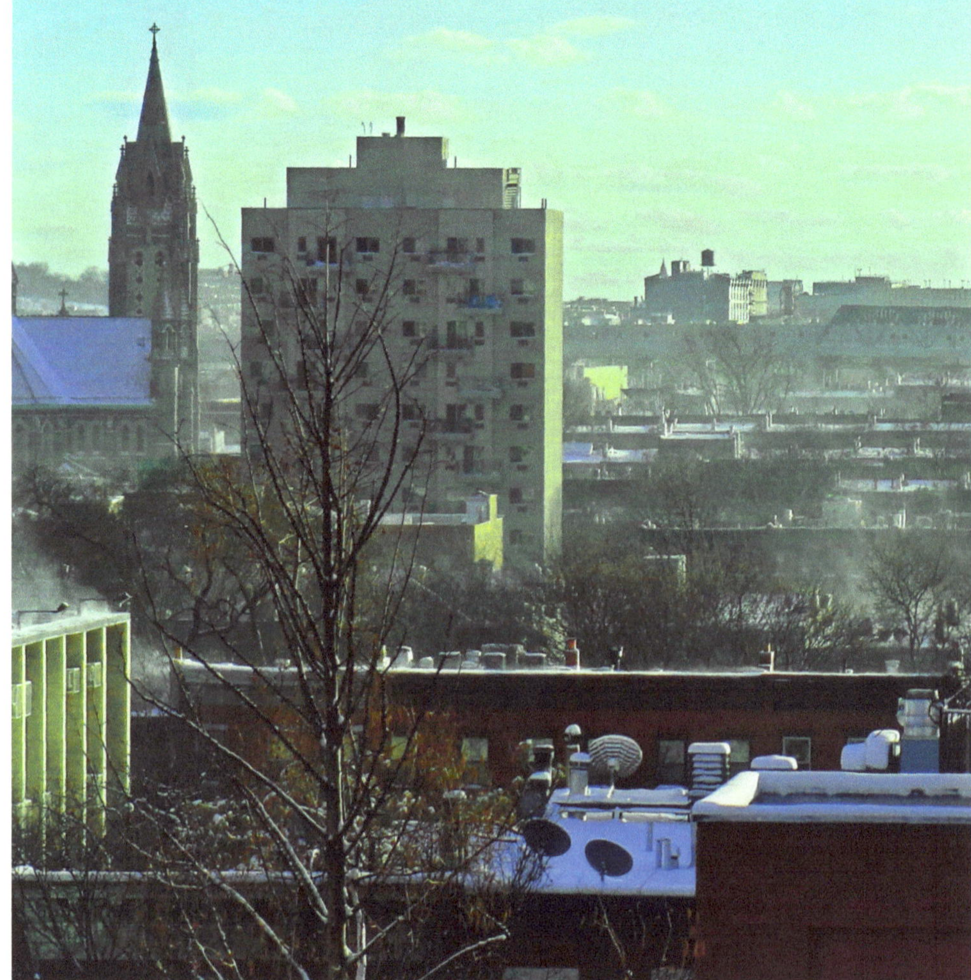

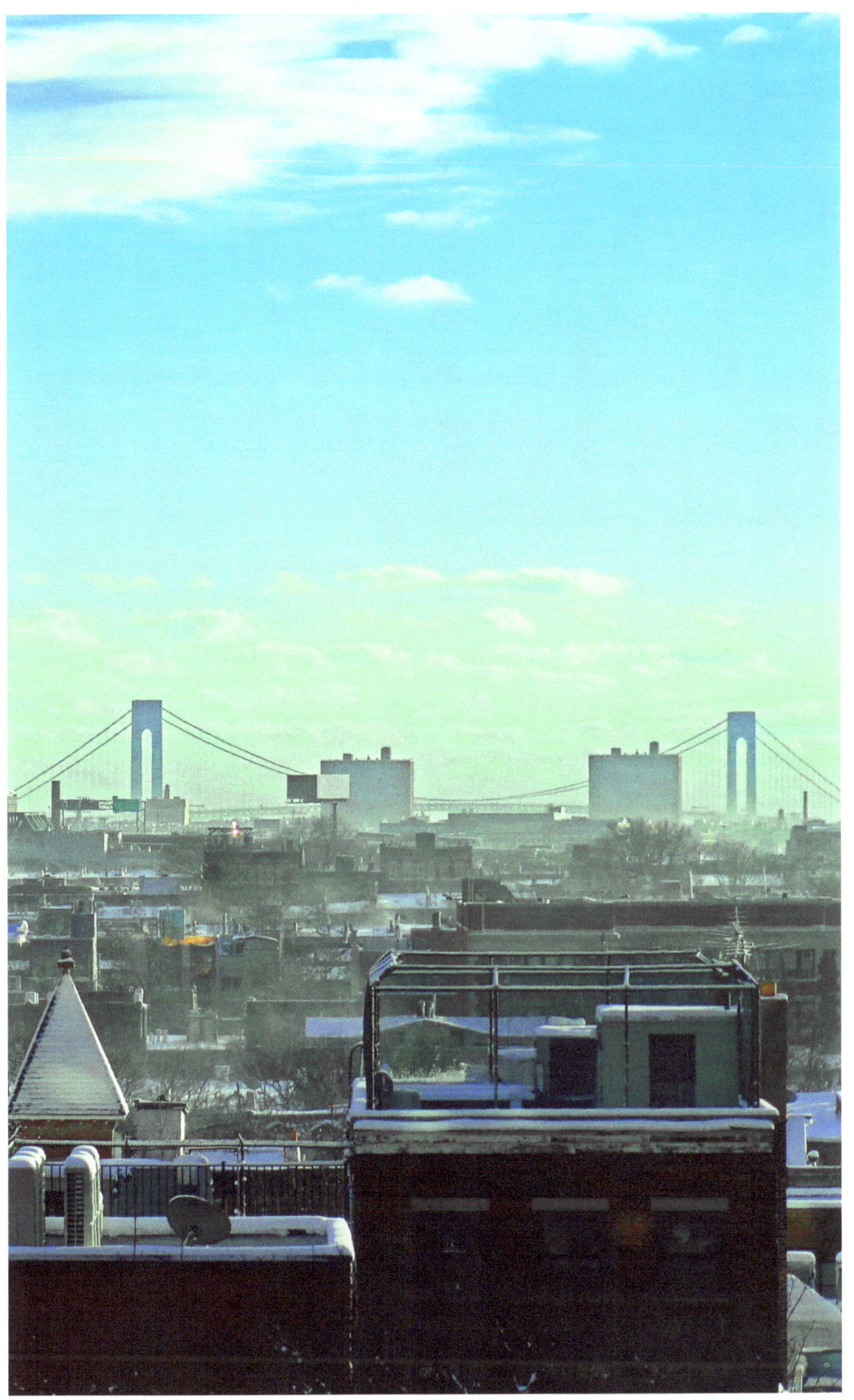

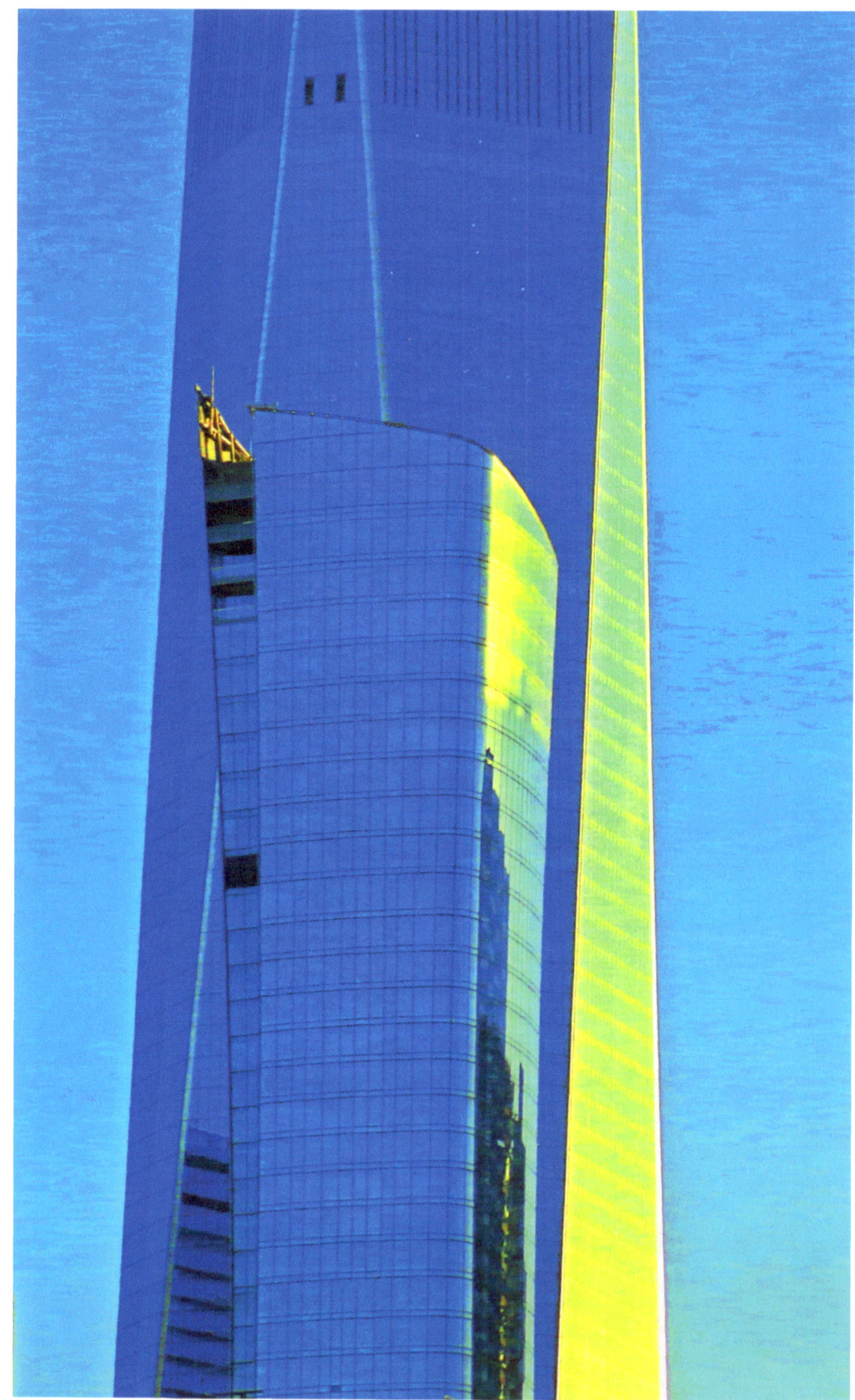

Mending Thread
   — for Phyllis and Diane

When I was young I said I would not pray,
I thought it quite absurd the world may change
miraculously at my flit request
and the Almighty do what I suggest.
Yet through the years I've thought a different way
and take the time to pause, reflect and pray
if to admit what little that I know
and give myself a chance to further grow
and with the modest means that I may give
thanks for the food I eat and place I live.
We are often torn and easily fray
so I take the time to reflect on grace,
little offerings of my somber breath
that softly stitch a tender, mending thread
and from a distance find a way to touch
a cherished life with kind and thoughtful love.

The Heart Rhymes with Redemption

I rise from my rest to a bright new day
but sadly, I keep turning my attention
to those parts of my life that were torn away.

Possibility opens in every way
spaciously awaiting any invention,
as I rise from my rest to a bright new day.

But I often hear sadness in what I say,
the past can be an entrapping condition
strewn with aching parts of my life torn away.

Other times there is nothing but wonder when I wake
as if sentience is its own validation
lighting up the skies of a bright new day.

The sun will shine, the rain will wash away,
with every beginning, there will be an end
releasing me from what was torn away.

All of those losses offer more than pain.
They are holes and hollows where we may extend.
In every morning there is a bright new day
where we may renew parts of our lives torn away.

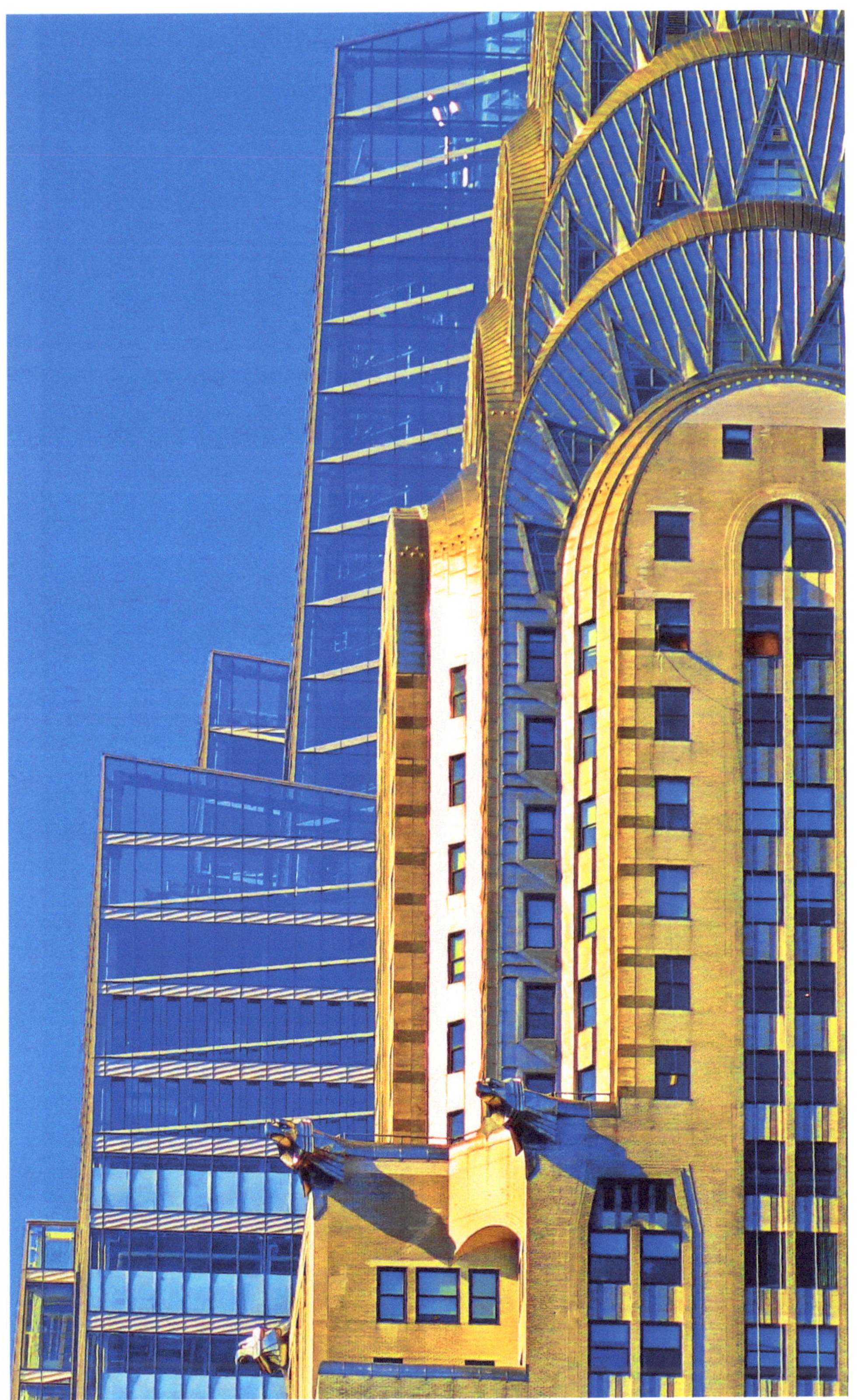

Torn Together

There is an odd sense of a mental storm
with conceptions projected from the mind.
Going out, the further in one is thrown,
then turning in, one finds oneself outside.
How can the whimsical notions of thought
shape the terrain of one's environment?
How can the settled place of one's own lot
become the source of one's own torment?
Can we make a ground that does not quake
or make a sky that never knows a storm?
Can we make a heart that does not break
or a fabric worn that is not shorn or torn?
Yet the sad, battered rafts on which we're born
are nature's way to keep us moving on.

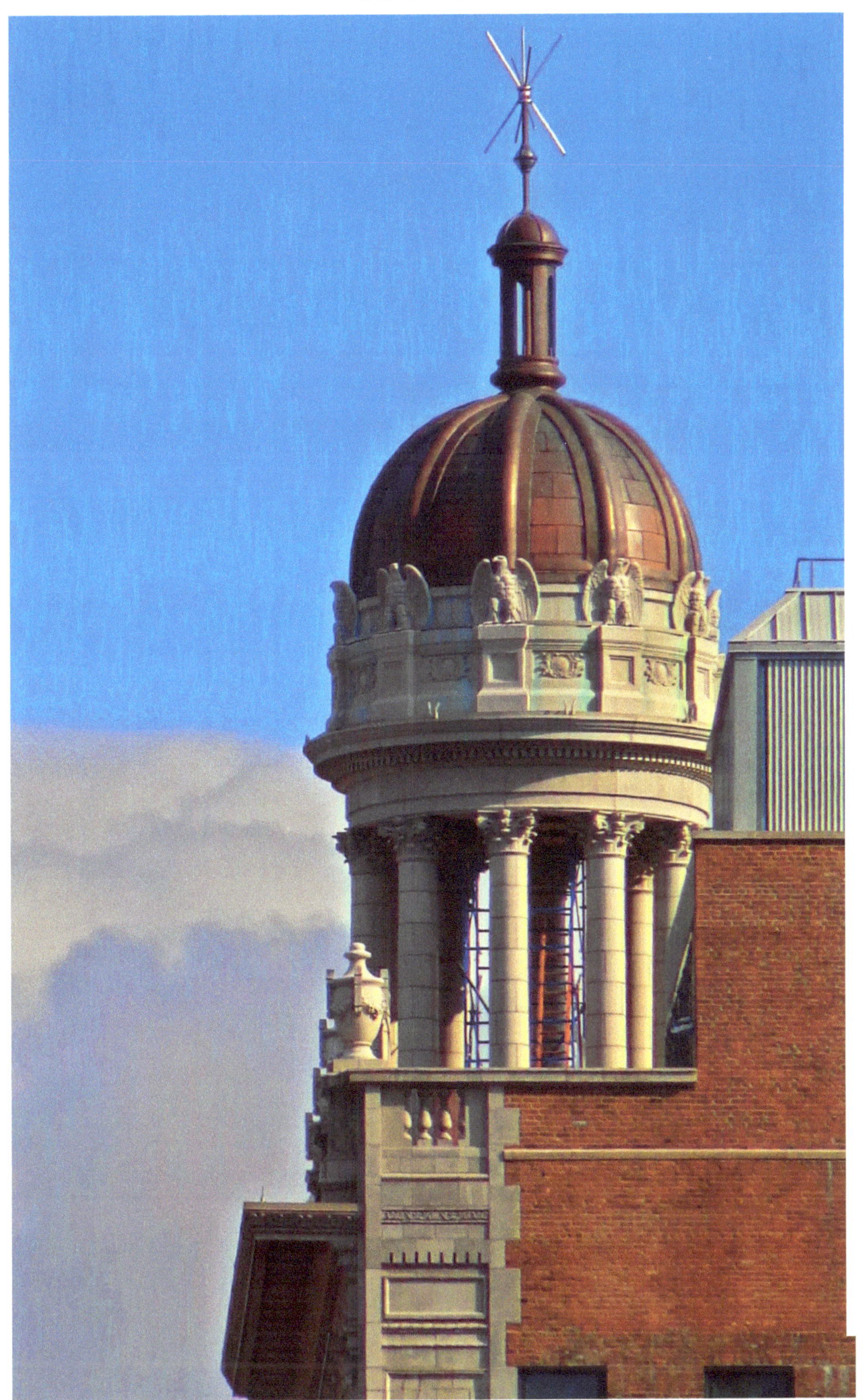

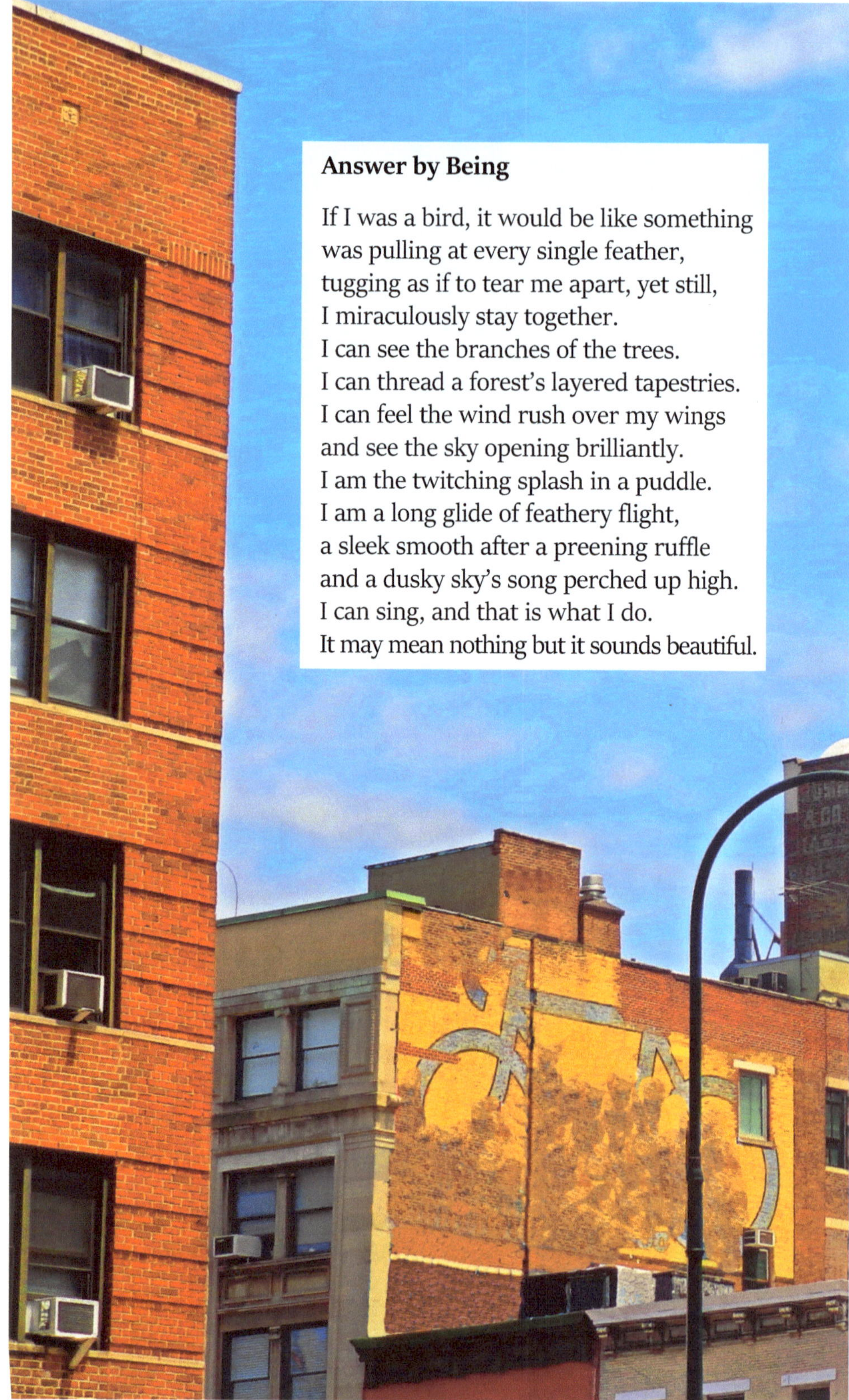

Answer by Being

If I was a bird, it would be like something
was pulling at every single feather,
tugging as if to tear me apart, yet still,
I miraculously stay together.
I can see the branches of the trees.
I can thread a forest's layered tapestries.
I can feel the wind rush over my wings
and see the sky opening brilliantly.
I am the twitching splash in a puddle.
I am a long glide of feathery flight,
a sleek smooth after a preening ruffle
and a dusky sky's song perched up high.
I can sing, and that is what I do.
It may mean nothing but it sounds beautiful.

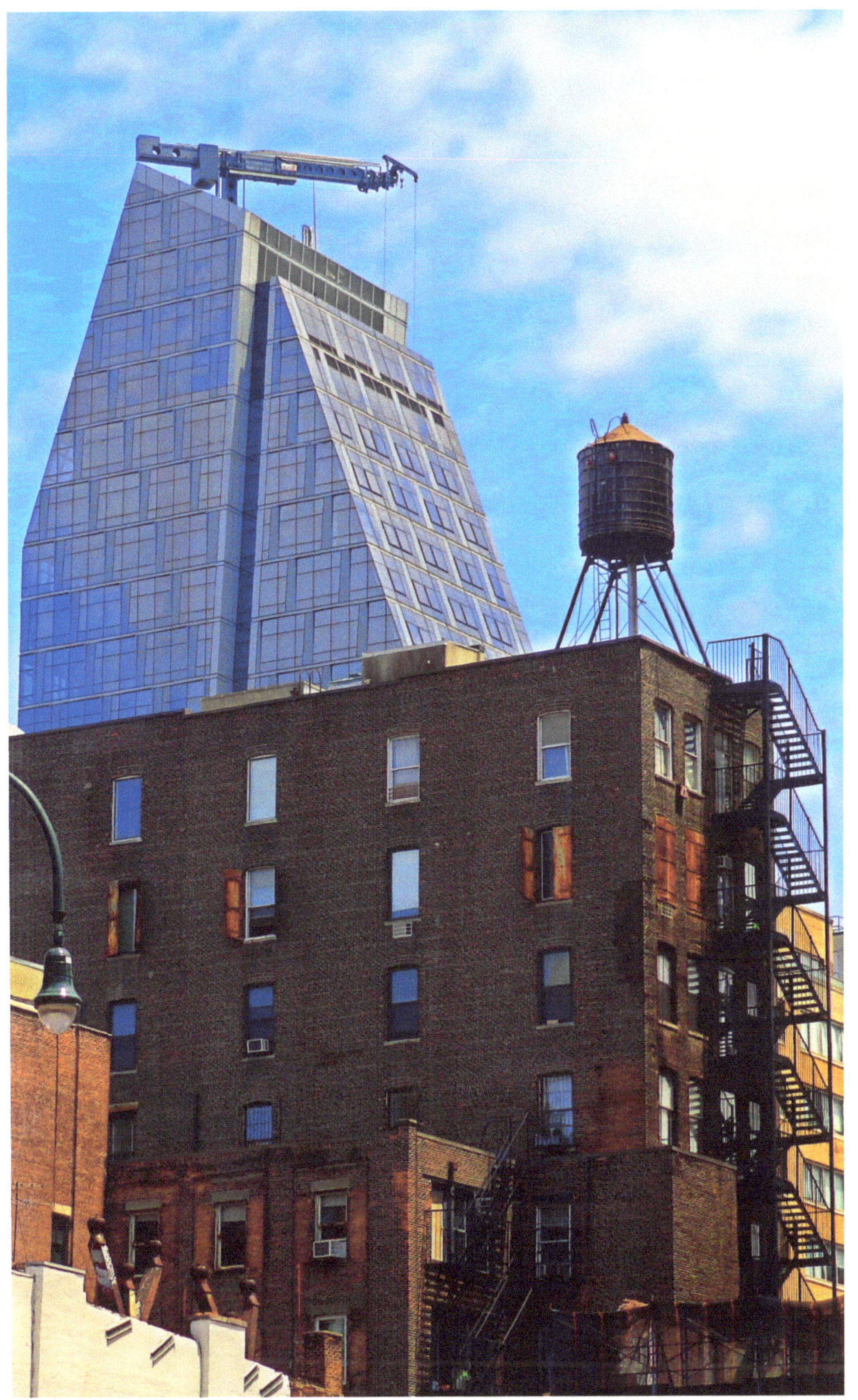

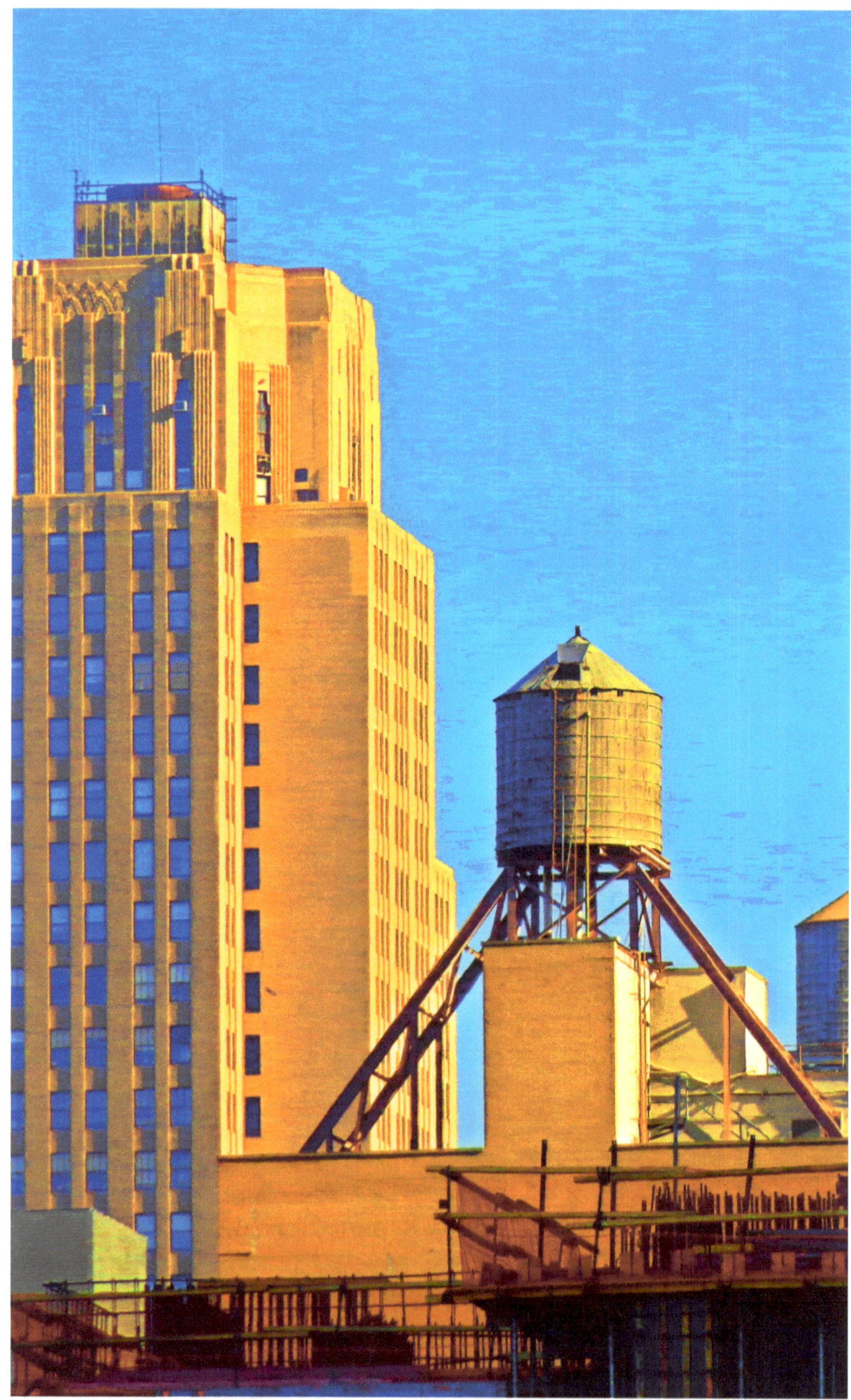

From the Surface of the Earth

Is there a way to push against nothing
and feel anything more than vacancy?
Yet space extends for an immensity
and what develops begins with something.

What is the bearing without direction?
The only way one knows how to respond
is simply to press oneself beyond
the meager means of one's limitations.

Is there a way to determine what one is
when one can only find oneself alone?
Yet what one is is one's own decision
beginning with knowing that one exists.

Perhaps one's gone too far and there's nothing left,
perhaps there is nothing more than emptiness
and this emptiness is what one must accept,
yet there is a stark beauty in this openness

and one can see possibilities expand
and one may go as far as one can.

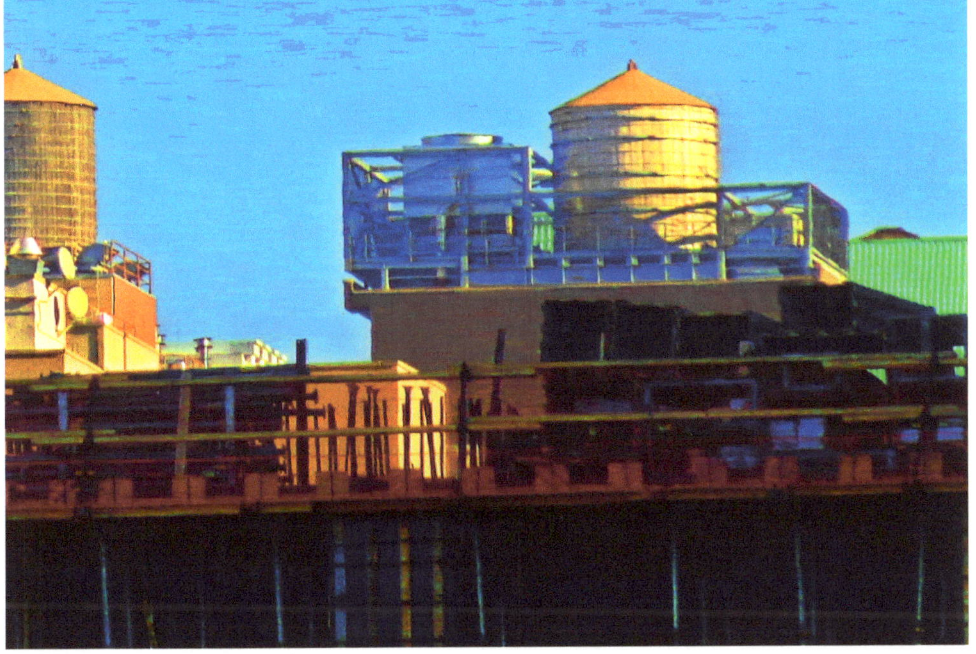

At the Steps of a Beaux Arts Building

"Of course my mother did not want me to leave,
— 'Let your father try to fly over the sea.'
She is made of love. Love is her essence
and the endlessness of her existence.
Yet love is not only security,
it also necessitates understanding.
Nothing that is loved can remain precious
else it spoil in coddled repression
and something mothers sadly understand
is the adventurous aims of a young man.

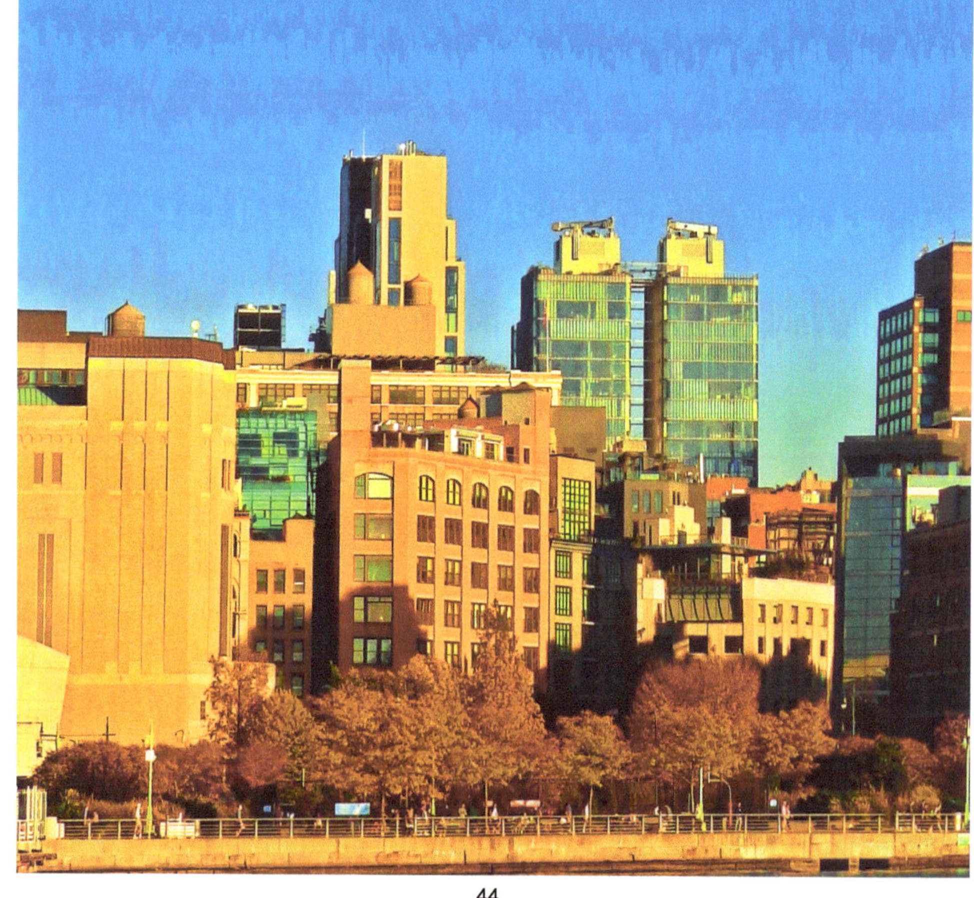

"My father always had a plan and his
mind is a vast labyrinth of ideas.
Unrolling scrolls of sketches on the table,
we would piece together and assemble
the intricacies of whimsical fancy
and construct them into tangible reality.
He said this time he had an insight
that would provide us the means to fly
and we dovetailed the joints of the whispery
frames to hoist our lives into the sky.
Candles burning through the late night hours
dripped sticky wax onto the papyrus
so the matted reeds could play the wind
and feather our frames with inspiration.

"Later, we awkwardly walked into the breeze
feeling how the frames flexed but kept their strength,
and with so much time laboring over them
they seemed to be natural appendages.

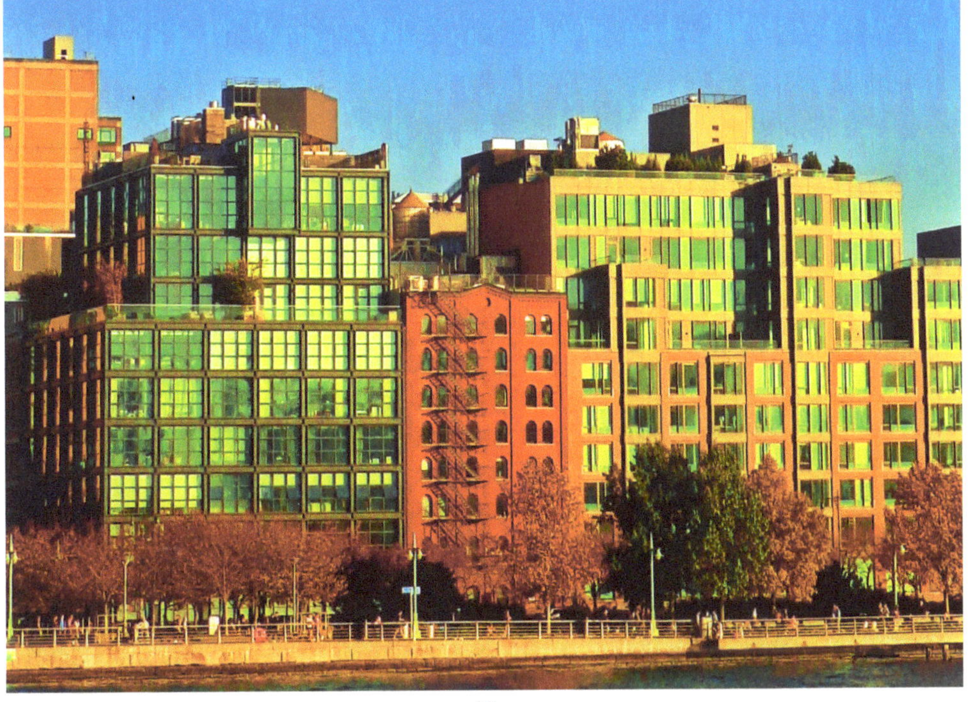

"Then peeking over the bleak precipice
my father told me to look up toward success
yet still he insisted that he would leap first,
confident, yet in case of the worst,
one of us could continue our work.

"Watching my father step into the open,
seemingly suspended upon nothing,
I was unsure what enabled him to fly —
his outstretched wings or his ecstatic surprise.
Then fluttering to catch the fresh wind's breath
and carry him further into the firmament
he looked back to wave me into the openness,
my courage emboldened with his success,
and released with uplifting victory
we flew together between the sun and sea.

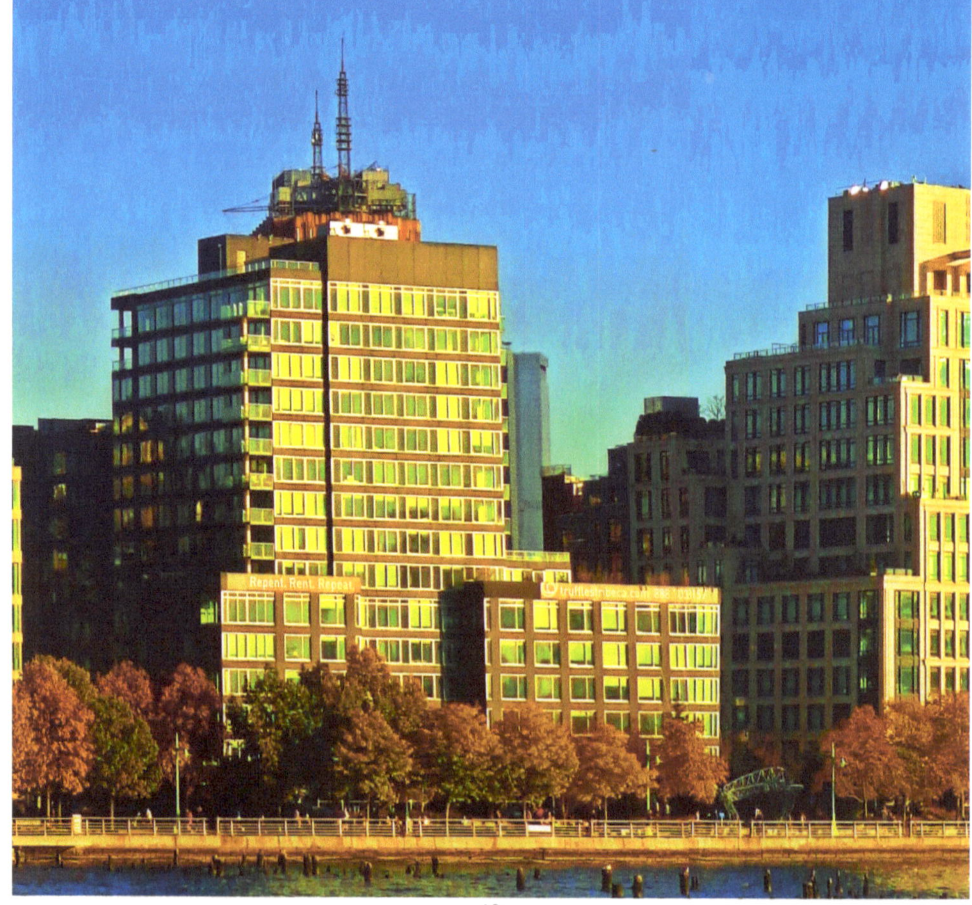

"Yet driven with my youthful temperament
I yearned for something more and different
and willed myself for a daring climb
to press how far and high I might rise.
My father yelled for me to refrain,
he had instructed we keep the middle way.
Yet nature nor reason can contain
when brazen youth has been enflamed —
why should I do what is most easily done
when I might climb up high to touch the sun?

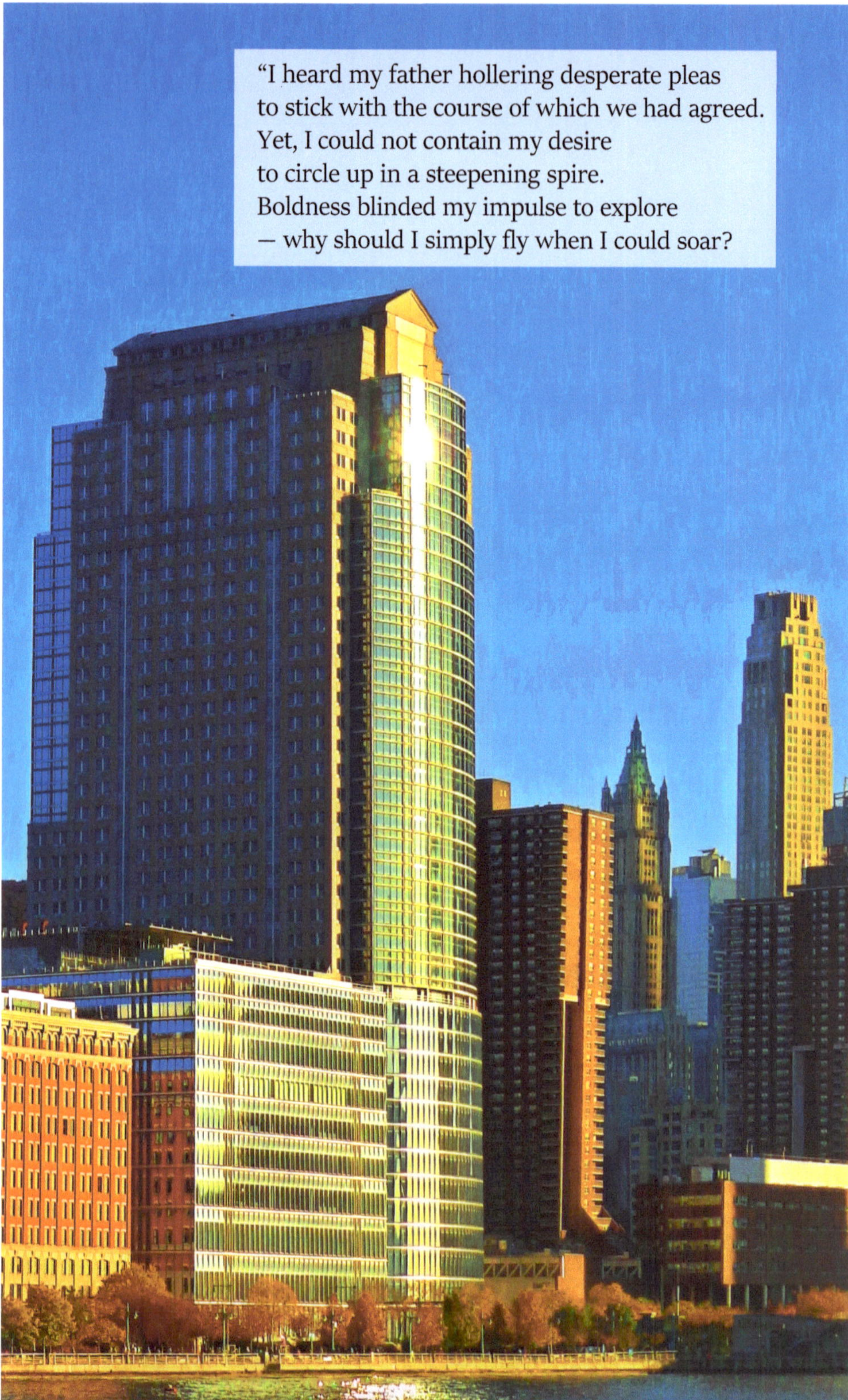

"I heard my father hollering desperate pleas
to stick with the course of which we had agreed.
Yet, I could not contain my desire
to circle up in a steepening spire.
Boldness blinded my impulse to explore
— why should I simply fly when I could soar?

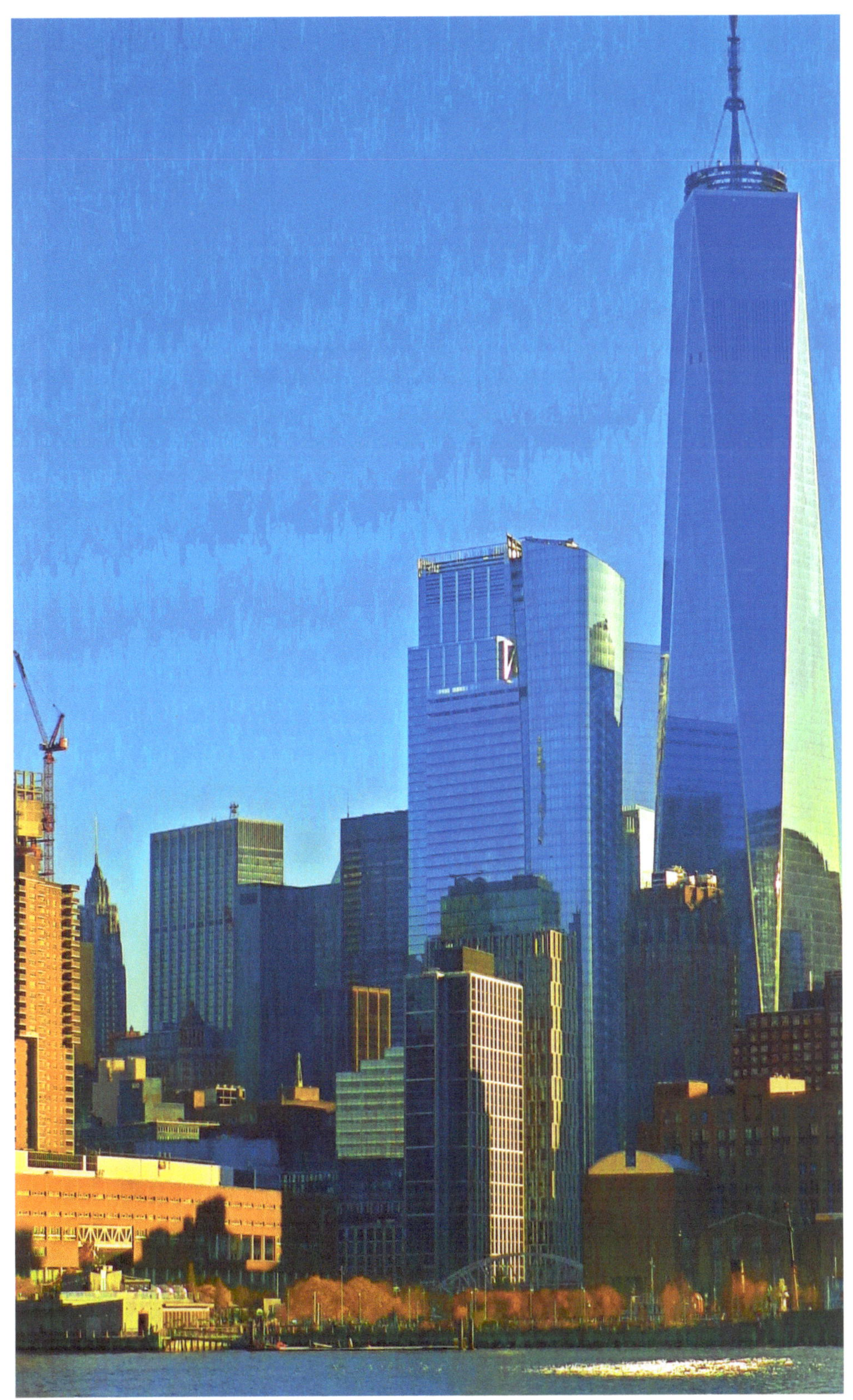

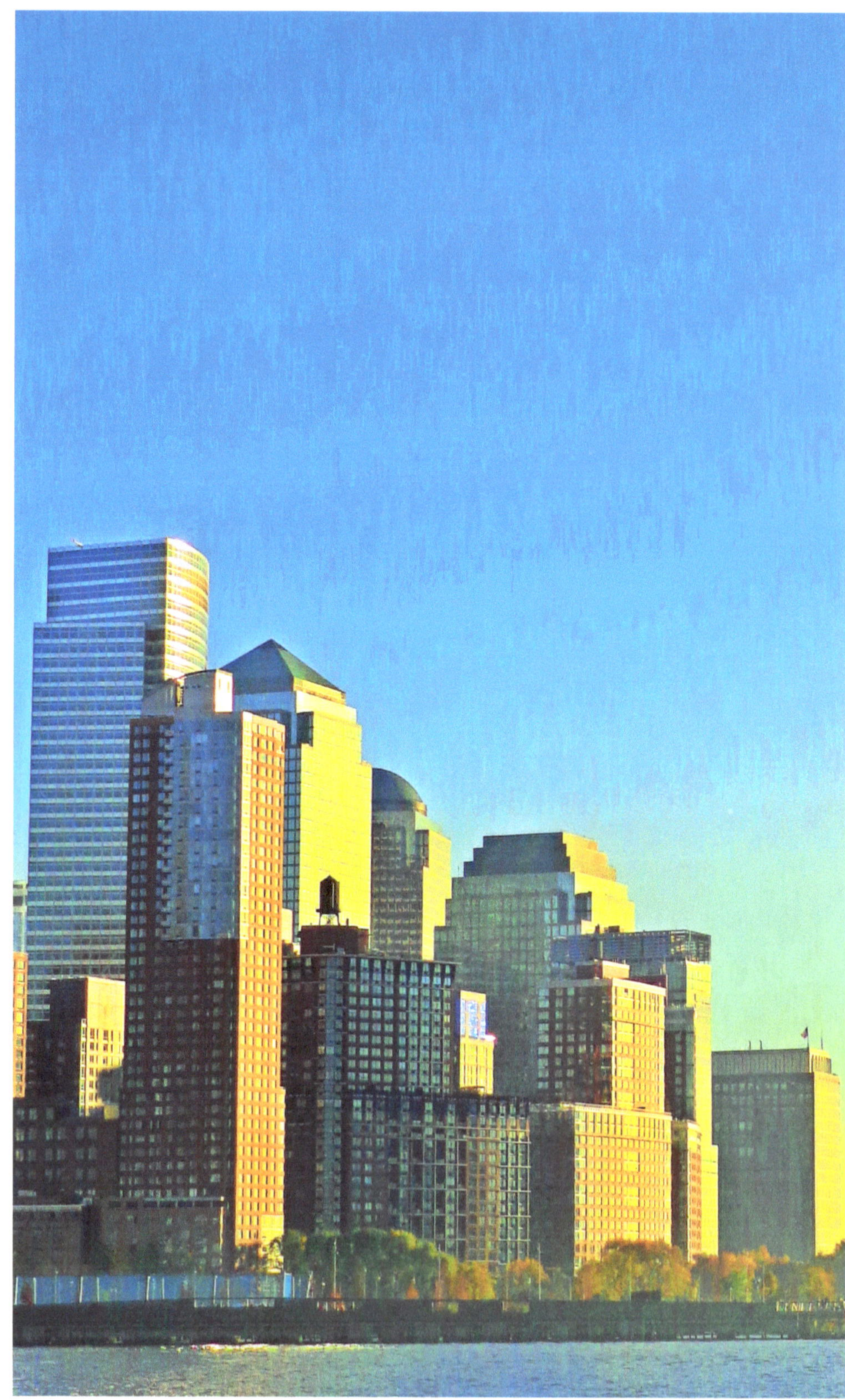

"And as I was assured by my father's call
those reckless ambitions are doomed to fall.
What could I expect to reward my daring feat?
The sun began to burn with searing heat,
melting the wax covering my wings
and the wind whistled as it passed through them
as if they were Winter trees' naked limbs.

"My father must have watched in horror,
forced to witness in helpless terror
as if his son had become the dead weight of a stone
plummeting to crash in the water below
and although my father would never abandon me
I had abandoned myself foolishly
and less we both be lost to the sea
he flew on to keep me in his memory.

"Now I know my father did succeed
and reached his goal triumphantly.
He landed on the shore of Sicily
and his fame continues to increase.
After I fell, if you are wondering,
although I could not fly, I could still swim
and although uncertain of my direction
I compensated with vigorous exertion
following the currents I was carried in
until I spotted land on the horizon
then I climbed through the surf's loudening roar."

— And that is when Icarus swam to shore.

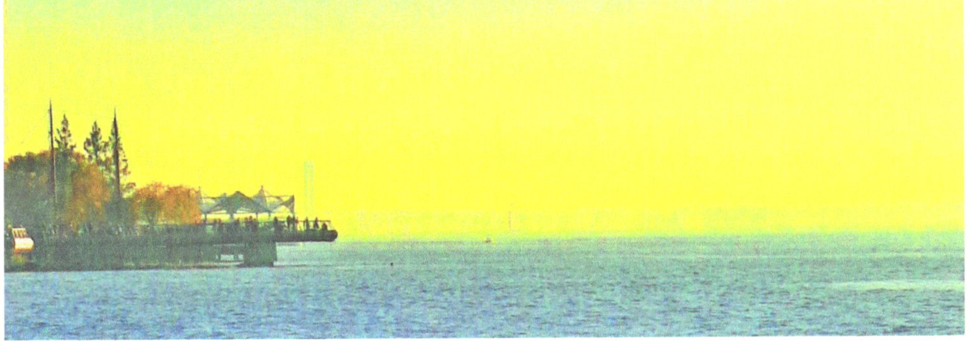

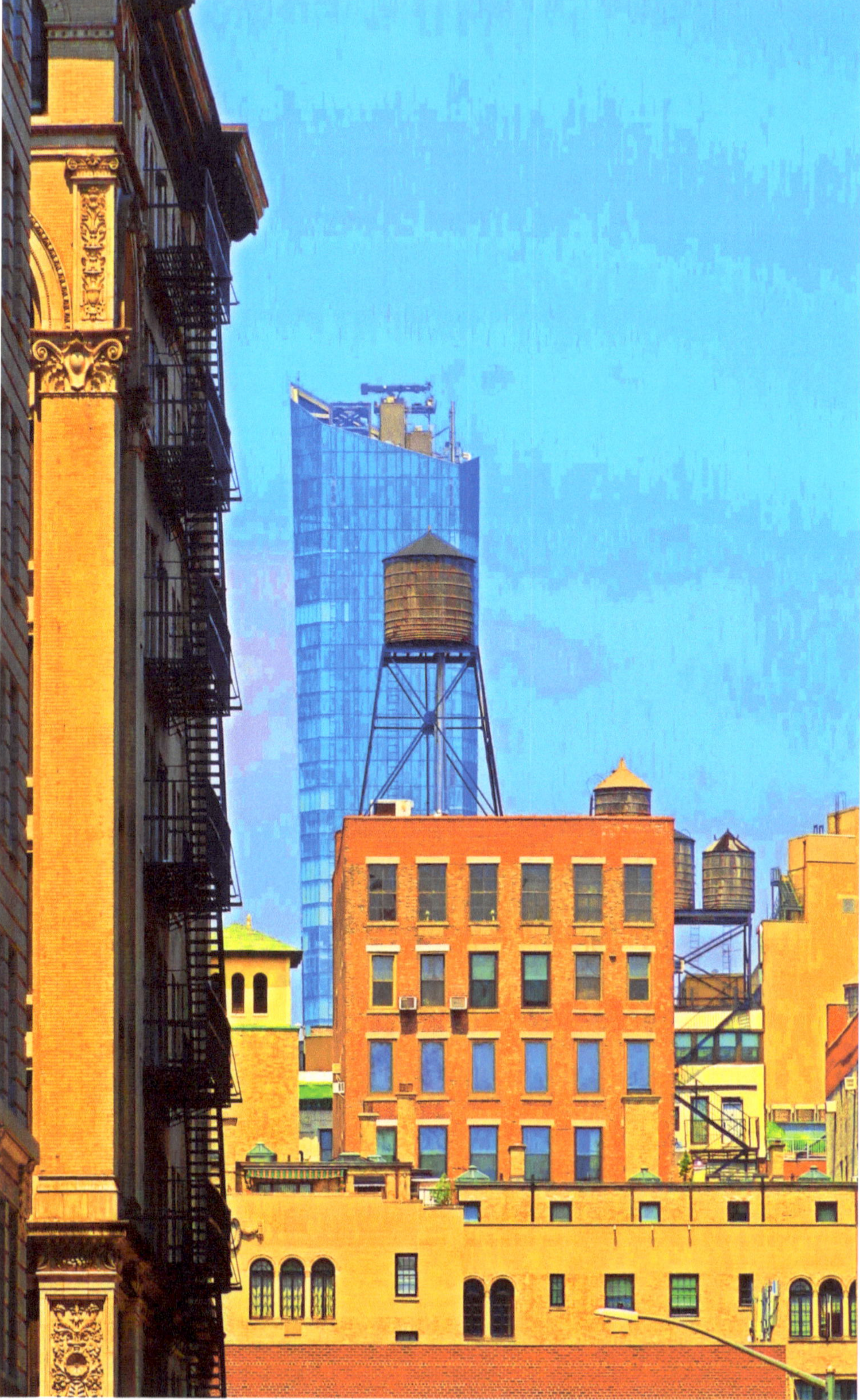

Poems and Buildings

I believe we can live in poems as we live in buildings. They provide a place where we may rest and renew, reflect and project.

From outside, they are mysterious as people filled with the personal and professional. Then stepping in, we can wonder how others have walked through these same passages, little steps of expressions that we share in common interests, the same phrases and arrangements read in the past and the present, another intersection of our lives that transcends time, space and status.

Peer through the windows opening in every direction, quickly peek to check the weather or stop to release pent up attention into the openness outside. The windows are little panes of glass, liquid waves within the frame — clear or opaque. Sometimes they are lenses magnifying the minute or telescoping distance. Sometimes they are little gazing gates where we may detach from the exact and wander off into thought. The drapes may be drawn at dawn, and in this, they can be the dawn, opening new days of novel interests. They can also open with the hush of the night, the soft, deepening dark filling with sparkling stars that beckon us to drift off into our dreams.

They are little places where we may drink from the refreshment of fountains, dine upon the delicacies of enriching sustenance and gather in conversations with voices through the ages.

They are inns where we may stop along our journeys. They are adorned with intriguing features of the locale and fashioned with amenities for soft pauses of comforting thoughts.

They are our homes from where we embark into each new day and return from our outgoing exchanges with the relaxing evening. We fill the corridors with arrangements of our interests assembled in delineations of space and situated for our personal tastes designated with the devotion of our attention.

Furnished with the familiar they give us rest where we may repair for the unexpected as we settle deeper within and extend further throughout in our ascents and descents of incremental steps like the notes of musical movement.

Garrett Buhl Robinson
November 1, 2020

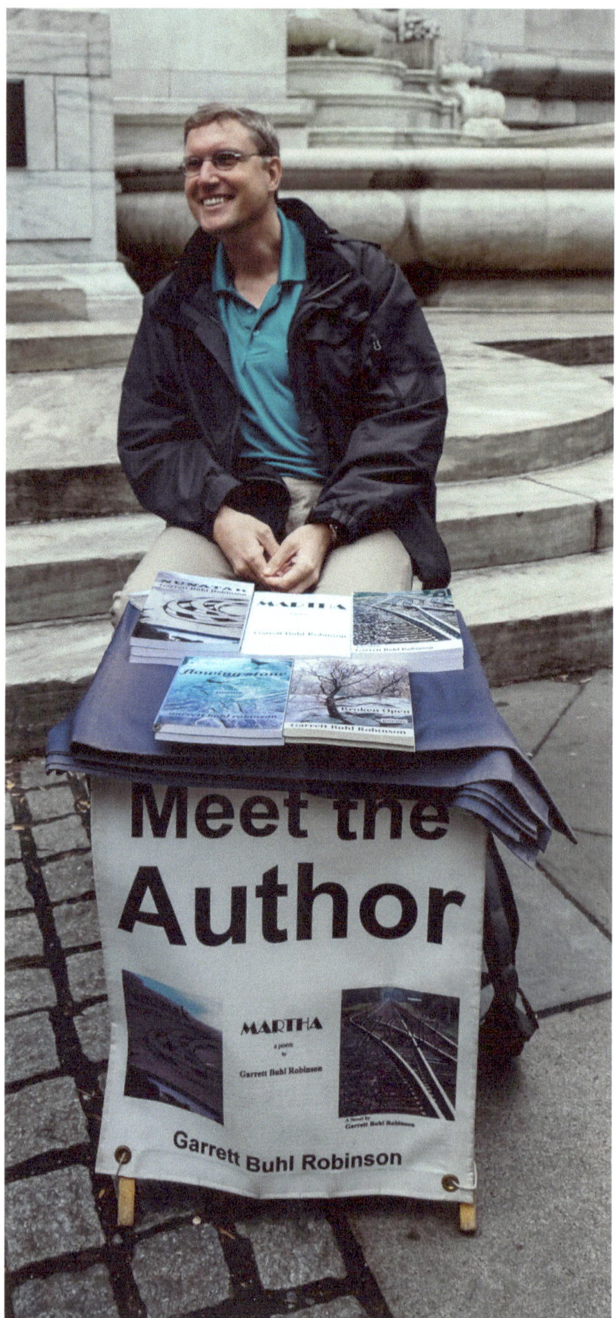

Meet the
Author
MARTHA
a poem
by
Garrett Buhl Robinson
Garrett Buhl Robinson

Some other titles by Garrett Buhl Robinson

<u>Poetry</u>

Pilgrims
Whispering Emily
Little Pieces of Poetry
A Man Who Lives in a Dream
The Ballad of Emperor Norton
The Nobody
Always Here Always Odd
Beauty beyond Reason
Martha, a poem

<u>Fiction</u>

Zoë
Nunatak

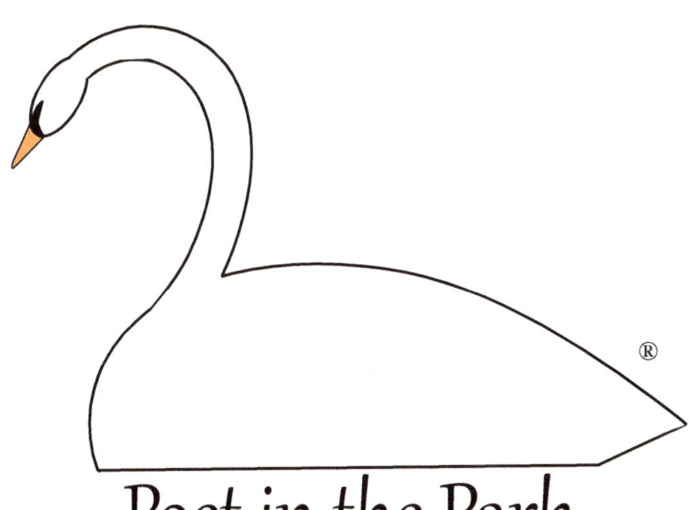

www.ingramcontent.com/pod-product-compliance
Lightning Source LLC
Chambersburg PA
CBHW041224050726
47599CB00001B/63